John Bunyan

– God's Tinker –

John Bunyan

– God's Tinker –

by

Robert M. Rosio

Christian ❖ Literature ❖ Crusade
Fort Washington, Pennsylvania 19034

CHRISTIAN LITERATURE CRUSADE
U.S.A.
P.O. Box 1449, Fort Washington, PA 19034

with publishing programs also in:
GREAT BRITAIN
51 The Dean, Alresford, Hants., SO24 9BJ

AUSTRALIA
P.O. Box 419M, Manunda QLD 4879

NEW ZEALAND
10 MacArthur Street, Feilding

ISBN 0-87508-462-1

Text set in Book Antiqua
Titles set in Oxford

Cover design by Nancy Watson

This printing 1999

Printed in the United States of America

Table of Contents

Introduction

Much of the true "nectar" of the "historical flower" is biographical. Crane Brinton declared that history is essentially an account of the behavior of men. I would expand Brinton's definition to say that history is essentially an account of the behavior of men *before God.*

God's favorite method for affecting the historical process is, I contend, to use men and women to accomplish His goals. And these particular men and women are all alike in that they are not self-made but are people who were handcrafted by God for purposes of His own. Because they are God's workmanship, there is something solid and weighty about their lives—something universal and eternal; something that inspires hope.

There are no shortcuts in God's painstaking artistic process. His first workings in a life are usually deep inner workings. He first establishes a strong root, which will later enable that life to bear good fruit. John Bunyan is an excellent example of God's artistic process. This specific process, profoundly changing his life, is what has made him such a blessing to so many others for so long.

Few people are remembered a hundred years after their death. Our memory of John Bunyan burns brightly three hundred years after his passing. I hope this book will help us all to understand why.

John Bunyan's contemporaries spoke of him as a tall, well-built man with long reddish-brown hair, a quick wit, and twinkling blue eyes. They also remembered him as a friendly and well-spoken (though clearly rustic) man. More than that, however, those who knew him personally—or perhaps primarily through his preaching and writing—were impressed by one thing above all others: his evangelistic heart.

The famed Bible teacher A. W. Tozer once said that *what a man thinks about God* is the most important thing about him and will determine the whole course of his life. Tozer's comment provides a key to understanding the heart and the mission of John Bunyan. Simply stated, Bunyan was a *God-intoxicated man,* a man on a mission. To understand the man and his mission a little more clearly will be the goal of this book.

The seventeenth-century world was dramatically different from the world in which we are now living. That was largely a theological age. In order to understand John Bunyan—the man and his mission—we must first understand something about the age in which he lived and enter into his religious worldview. (We shall mine those two historical veins later on.)

If I am correct about Bunyan being, after his spiritual awakening, a man on a mission, it should be helpful at this point to look at what his mission was. We can use this knowledge as a lens through which to more closely inspect his life and motivation.

In truth, Bunyan had a dual mission. The first part of his mission was to pursue God in His Word in order to find assurance of his own eternal salvation. This all-consuming quest is described in his spiritual autobiography *Grace Abounding to the Chief of Sinners.* Bunyan himself stated that sound doctrine "starts from the necessity of having God break the heart in order to bring salvation." In short, his message to all men was "repent, believe, and love." The second aspect of his mission (which might indeed more properly be called a "commission," according to the definition given in Matthew 28:18–20 and Mark 16:15) was to tell all those he could—all those who would read or listen to his words—the story of God's righteousness, mankind's need for a Savior, and God's offer of salvation through Jesus Christ.

Biographer Ola Elizabeth Winslow has written of Bunyan that "one does not live with him very long in his many treatises and sermons without being struck by the singleness of purpose that runs through everything that he wrote or spoke. Eternal salvation and how to get it was his lifelong theme. Nearly everything in his life proceeded from this one challenge." Bunyan was successful at his task because salvation was so personal to him and because the right to speak and write about it had been obtained at such a great cost. He desired to communicate to others the message of God's grace that he had found so clearly communicated in the New Testament.

Somewhat like the apostle Paul, whose days in prison enabled him to find both time and motivation to write the epistles that were the crowning glory of all his inspired writings, Bunyan's imprisonment led to the writing of many spiritual works—over sixty in all—including his masterpiece, *The Pilgrim's Progress.* This book, born of intense soul-searching, personal conviction, and Bible study, is perhaps the most famous allegory every written. It remains to this day one of the most widely read books in all of human history. It is the legacy of a simple man, a "mechanick" preacher (one of the class of self-taught Puritan preachers who worked with their hands to support their preaching) who wished to tell the world about the good news that had so changed his life, so inspired his heart, and now motivated his spiritual pilgrimage.

Monica Furlong writes that "the idea of the salvific journey was a commonplace of seventeenth-century theology—it appeared in innumerable sermons and books of pious instruction. What Bunyan did was to take up this commonplace idea and transform it with imagination and deep psychological insight, born of his own terrible experience. His beliefs were so thoroughly assimilated that they did not clash with the artistic purpose of the book, in fact they gave it its passion and energy."

The concept of "being a pilgrim" is currently unfamiliar to many Americans. There is a twofold reason for this. The first is that most Americans (unlike most Englishmen of Bunyan's time) are not students of the Bible. The second is that most Americans have little appreciation for history. The story of our Pilgrim fathers has largely disappeared from American history books, their heroic sacrifice having often been written out of the texts. One textbook identifies "pilgrims" simply as "people who go on long trips." Bunyan, who certainly considered himself to be a pilgrim in the biblical sense of the word, detailed his own "long trip" in the world's most famous allegory, *The Pilgrim's Progress.*

The book of Revelation divides the human race into two categories: those who are "heaven dwellers" and those who are "earth dwellers." The first group see their true home as heaven: they have an eternal outlook. The second see their true home as earth: they are time-bound. The first group see themselves as simply *passing through* the time period and realm in which they were born; they are not rooted in the temporary here-and-now. They are *pilgrims*—people simply passing through, on their way to a better place and fulfilling a higher calling.

It is no surprise that earth dwellers understand only with great difficulty those who consider themselves to be "pilgrims"—if indeed they can understand them at all. Such was the case with many who met John Bunyan. The authorities looked upon him with suspicion, believing that he was preaching sedition. They thought that his preaching was somehow "political," though it decidedly was not *intended* to be. Bunyan believed he was called to preach God's good news, a revelation that had little to do with English politics—although religion and politics were actually very closely intertwined at that time. It is hard for those of us who have become so profoundly shaped by the concept of the separation of church and state to understand this. It was inescapable that religion would have political implications.

Bunyan, like the apostle Paul before him, saw his calling as preaching God's pure word of salvation. It was out of this calling that his writing ministry naturally grew. His sermons have mostly passed away, as have most of his polemical writings—theological works in which he inveighed against what he considered to be spiritual error among his contemporaries. Yet the essential Bunyan remains, recorded for all to read in his two greatest works: *Grace Abounding to the Chief of Sinners* and *The Pilgrim's Progress.* The latter completes in the form of an allegory the personal story of Bunyan's spiritual pilgrimage explained in the former. Other notable works of his are: *The Holy War* and *The Life and Death of Mister Badman.*

The Pilgrim's Progress, still shining brightly across the centuries, is the simple story of a dedicated pilgrim on life's most important pilgrimage: the journey to find the way to God . . . to find eternal salvation . . . to find one's way to his eternal home. This is the reason why John Bunyan is so important to readers in all ages (but perhaps especially important to those in our present biblically-illiterate times). The story of John Bunyan is the story of Everyman. As Vera Brittain has said, "By his writings he revealed himself as the interpreter of not only his own age but of the human spirit in all ages."

Chapter One

The Early Years

It may seem strange for those of us living in the Information Age—we who are so accustomed to the minute scrutiny of the lives of celebrities—to learn that history knows so very little about the early life of a man as famous as John Bunyan. Yet it is true. His early years remain quite obscure, and what we know for certain about the young Bunyan can be summed up in a few short paragraphs.

John Bunyan was born in 1628 outside the village of Elstow, England, near Bedford (about 45 miles north of London). Elstow had a rich historic past, dating back to the time of the Romans. Although history does not record the exact date of John's birth, we know that he was baptized on November 30 in a church that dates back to the time of William the Conqueror. In the first half of the seventeenth century, the church exercised strict control over the life of every Englishman. Parents were compelled to have their children baptized. Vera Brittain writes that "the Reverend Thomas Kellie, Vicar of Elstow, christened him on November 30. In the parish register, when the brief ceremony was over, the vicar entered the baby's name as 'John the sonne of Thomas and Margaret Bonnionn.' Then he closed the book, his mind untroubled by the remote contingency that the name he had written would become immortal. For him, it was only another village christening."

Bunyans had lived in the Bedford area for three hundred years. John's father, Thomas, was a brazier (commonly called a "tinker" in those days). He was, however, a landed, not a roving tinker. A tinker in seventeenth-century England was a type of handyman: he repaired pots and pans and was often capable of a wide range of domestic repair jobs. Thomas Bunyan was the first member of his family to follow this craft.

No doubt due to economic necessity, the young John Bunyan received only a rudimentary education. It is assumed that he attended a grammar school in Bedford or somewhere nearby. Bunyan later wrote that "it pleased God to put it into my parents' hearts to put me in school to learn both to read and write." He added that "I did soon lose the bit I learnt . . . long before the Lord did His gracious work of conversion of my soul." Biographer Ola Elizabeth Winslow, however, makes an important point regarding Bunyan's schooling. She states, "Blessedly he had learned to read, and the key was in his hand. It would open many doors, most importantly of all for him, doors to the knowledge of the Bible."

The Bible advises us not to despise the day of small beginnings. Bunyan's scant education gave him a priceless gift: the ability to read.

Bunyan's parents, like most working-class people, had been trained from their youth in Bible reading and prayer. John, however, much preferred to read adventure stories. He was especially fond of stories drawn from the tales of chivalry. He later wrote that, at that time, "for the Holy Scriptures I cared not." In future years, however, spiritual hunger would cause him to make God's book his own. Ms. Winslow comments that "the Bible would be to him a school and college education; in fact, almost a total culture." Vera Brittain adds that "he knew the Bible so intimately that at every turn of every road its words were a lamp unto his feet and a light unto his path."

It seems likely that John left school in order to learn the trade of his father. Like him, he would become a tinker. His lack of much early formal education determined to a degree the course his life would follow. He would first become a "mechanick" (a man who worked with his hands) and later a "mechanick preacher" (one of the many Puritan preachers who followed manual trades to support their families while they preached the Word of God). The apostle Paul had been a tentmaker. Bunyan was a tinker, a small-town tinker.

Mechanick preachers like John Bunyan frequently aroused great hostility among the educated classes in England. These preacher's words were, nonetheless, a powerful expression of the growing concepts of the time. Such men took on new importance and significance. In matters of Scripture they often became the equal of any man in England. Their faith in God and in His Word gave a new identity, confidence, and dignity to a whole class of people: the poor. The tremendous potential for change in society that this implied was not lost upon the upper classes. The understanding that God's grace was available to all (and especially the fact that all men might preach this good news) leveled the playing field in many ways. The rich were of no more importance in God's economy than were the poor.

John Bunyan remained true to his humble roots all his life. Biographer Christopher Hill observes that "Bunyan is the first major English writer who was neither London-based nor university trained." In reality, during all his life and despite all of his fame, he seldom wandered far from home. Roger Sharrock has written that Bunyan "is the greatest representative of the common people to find a place in English literature." What is that place? Henri A. Talon has described it this way: "He shared the fervor of his time, speaking with the voice of the 17th-century workingman. His work is the expression of the popular culture."

Bunyan himself wrote that during his youth he followed wild ways and had wild companions. He not only had little time for religion but he was famed for his swearing and lying. He describes himself as "the ringleader of all the youth that kept me company in all manner of vice and ungodliness." Biographer Gwilym O. Griffith depicts Bunyan as "something of an irrepressible little gypsy. He had his sports and playmates and the open country, and there was a wind on the heath." He also had the firm friendship and constant companionship of his sister, Margaret, fifteen months his junior. Together they fished in the Ouse River, sometimes from a boat, sometimes from the bank. On one of these fishing expeditions, young John fell out of the boat in a display of youthful exuberance—as well as of a youthful lack of caution—and barely managed to get himself back to shore.

In the brooks which ran into the Ouse, John and Margaret often gathered safer prey: minnows in a bucket. They passed many summer days this way, minnowing or fishing with a lunch of bread and cheese in their fishbasket. They also went exploring—tramping through the nearby fields, meadows and woods—looking for wild flowers and observing the many varieties of birds. It was a bright and sunny life in many ways. At the same time, however, there was also a shadow which fell across his young life: John sometimes had bad dreams. He writes that "after I had spent the day in sin, I was often greatly afflicted while asleep with the apprehensions of devils and wicked spirits." He also had experiences that could only be called some sort of "visitation." These visitations terrified him periodically, from the age of nine or ten until he was about twenty-five. Sometimes they even came upon him during the daylight hours. When they did, he was obliged to stop during his games with Margaret and other companions in order to find a place where he could be alone (sometimes behind a hedge or even in a ditch) until they passed. Perhaps the dreams and visitations were portents of the spiritual struggles to come.

John Bunyan's childhood came to an abrupt end in 1644. In June a strange illness swept over their little village. Before the end of the month, his mother died. Shortly afterwards, Margaret, his fourteen-year-old sister, his faithful and beloved companion, also died. Young John was heartbroken by this double blow of misfortune. And he was very upset when his father, ever the practical man, remarried almost immediately. Feeling alienated, upset, and lonely, the young man was grateful to soon have the opportunity to leave home. He was about to be caught up in the great national events of the Civil War.

Vera Brittain writes that "suddenly drums and trumpets began to sound all over England, and men were riding post-haste to battle. Half the combatants, rallying to the King's standard, wore feathered hats and long curls falling over the collars of the rich cloaks that covered their armor. The other half were distinguished only by their close-cropped heads and the sober hue of doublet and hose. Both sides believed that they were fighting for the welfare of their country." John decided that he would join his friends and neighbors in the Puritan army of Oliver Cromwell, fighting against the King. But he first had to persuade the recruiting soldiers that he was sixteen. This was not difficult for the tall, well-built, and confident fifteen-year-old. Brittain describes him in this way: "He was a tall, vigorous youth with large bones, a long stride, and a heavy tread. Even as a conscript among other conscripts, his dynamic energy, keen blue eyes, and abundant auburn hair no doubt made even the sober Parliamentary officers look at him twice."

Chapter Two

A Short History Lesson

John Bunyan was born in 1628 and died in 1688. His life thus bracketed the two English Civil Wars (wars which the famed Puritan poet John Milton called "the wars of truth"). Biographer Roger Sharrock wrote that Bunyan's story is hence "the story of the militant phase of English Puritanism, and its heroic struggle against persecution." Vera Brittain states that "the individual struggle for freedom of conscience, which carried John into prison for over a decade, mirrored in personal terms the national struggle for liberty of thought, speech, and worship which brought seven years of Civil War to England, and reached its climax with the execution of a king. The Puritan Revolution assumed a double character. On the political side it became a contest between King and Parliament for power. As a religious movement it became a struggle between orthodox Anglicans and unorthodox Puritans for the establishment of their respective forms of worship." As for Bunyan, "he was the individual who established through the political confusion and religious persecution, the right to maintain a direct relationship between himself and God. This lonely Puritan traveler symbolizes the unique contribution of the seventeenth century to the turbulent English past. To him we owe that freedom of worship which the English-speaking world has never forfeited."

Puritanism was more of a mindset, more of a way of life, than it was a specific religious practice. Originally, the term "Puritan" was a term of derision. It was coined around 1563 to describe those who believed that the reforms in the church during the reign of Elizabeth I had not gone far enough. The battle even then centered on questions of worship and church government. The Puritans advocated a type of Calvinism based upon the Genevan model. (Geneva, Switzerland, was the adopted home of the French theologian John Calvin.) They wanted to have the churches elect their own ministers and then have the ministers elect a general assembly. The most important development from the time of the exile of the Puritans under the reign of the Catholic queen Mary until the Civil War was the gradual growth of a school of preachers and pastors whose intellectual center was in Cambridge. In some ways, they were worthy successors to the Lollards in the time of John Wycliffe (1320–1384), who went forth throughout England preaching God's Word and were persecuted for doing so. At any rate, it was during the Elizabethan period that the term "Puritan" ceased to have a derogatory meaning.

Puritanism (the heart of Protestantism in England) was comprised of diverse groups, but these groups had several important things in common. They were Calvinistic in theology for the most part. They believed that the Bible was the inspired, authoritative, and infallible Word of God—their personal and corporate guide for holy living—and that individual conscience (as inspired by Scripture) was much more important in worship than rote, ritual, or state regulations. Bible expositor Martyn Lloyd-Jones has described them as "scrupulous in their desire to know exactly what the Truth is, not simply that they might have a theoretical knowledge of it, but in order that they might carry it out, and put it into practice, whatever the cost." And there was indeed a cost to be paid. True sons and daughters of the Reformation, they were not satisfied with correct doctrine but were intensely interested in holy living. To them, sermons based upon God's Word were literally a case of life and death. The roots of Puritanism go back as far, perhaps, as Tyndale's translation of the Bible into English in 1524.

Seventeen years before John Bunyan was born, the King James version of the Bible was published in 1611. Ola Elizabeth Winslow writes that in the first quarter of the seventeenth century "only the sailing of the *Mayflower* and the founding of the Plymouth colony are historical events commensurate in importance with the putting of this version of the Scriptures in the cottages of England. It would become the household book of the land. It would be read by the rank and file as it had never been read before and has never been read since. It would be the literal voice of God to individual men and women. It certainly was to John Bunyan."

William Tyndale had paid with his life for his ambition to put the Bible within popular reach. Tyndale had remarked that one day plowboys would know more of the Bible than did theologians of his day in England. "In a very true sense John Bunyan was one of Tyndale's plowboys," declares Ms. Winslow.

The primary Puritan emphasis was on God's grace and on correct pastoral theology. Puritans rejected both the concept of the divine right of monarchs to rule and the authority of the state church upon which the monarchy depended. From Queen Elizabeth (1533–1603) onward, Parliament became more and more Puritan in sentiment and in practice. Conflicts between Puritan Parliament and the kings James I (1603–1625) and Charles I (1625–1649) grew continually more bitter. It was clear that England was heading for Civil War.

When Oliver Cromwell, who in many ways represented the true Puritan spirit, led the forces of Puritan Parliament into war against their king, Charles I, he believed that they were waging war to gain three things. The first two were religious and political liberty. The third was a hope of founding a godly society in England—a society that would be based upon godly principles, thus guaranteeing God's blessing upon their nation. Roger Sharrock states that "the ideal aim of the Puritans was to make use of the power of the state to confirm their authority over men's souls and conduct."

We often hear it said that morality cannot be legislated (even if immorality can). The Puritans did not believe that. They felt that the true role of government was to serve God. They were strangers to the concept of separation of church and state. It must be remembered, however, that they lived (unlike us) in a theological age. Dr. Lloyd-Jones has described the Puritans as "men who were God-conscious, dominated by a sense of the presence of God. They were God-pleasers, not men-pleasers." Their zeal and their convictions made them uncompromising, unyielding, and inflexible in the causes they held dear.

History records that Cromwell won the war. It also records that Puritanism did not win the heart of the nation. Although Puritanism prevailed for a season, its control of society was short-lived. For one thing, the rigorous moral demands of the Puritans were not greatly appreciated by most Englishmen. In the end, they cried out for a return of the monarchy. When Oliver Cromwell died in 1658, the Puritan hopes of a society based upon godly principles died with him.

With the monarchy the state church returned. By 1662 the Puritans realized that they no longer had any hope of reforming the English church or English society. They had two basic choices: emigrate or endure. Each course was followed by many Puritans. Bunyan was one who chose to endure. However, unlike Oliver Cromwell, who wanted to politically reform the nation along theological lines, Bunyan saw his mission as being to preach the simple but powerful gospel by which individuals could come to eternal salvation.

Charles II reentered London on May 29, 1660. The restoration of the former state church system was immediately implemented by Edward Hyde and Lord Clarendon. Under the Act of Uniformity, it became illegal not to use the Church of England prayer book. The law also stipulated that anyone preaching the gospel must be ordained by Anglican bishops. Those who sought to preach the word in England were required to recognize the right and power of the King and Parliament to govern the church. This, of course, John Bunyan could not do—guided as he was by a conscience enlightened by Scripture. Within six months of Charles' return, Bunyan was beginning the first term of his twelve years of imprisonment.

3
Chapter Three

Bunyan: Soldier and Husband

A decree had gone out from Oliver Cromwell that all healthy men between the ages of sixteen and sixty were to report for military duty. Parliament was in urgent need of men. Cromwell himself had made several trips to the Bedford area to recruit men. Earlier, Royalist troops had made several raids in the Bedford area, seeking provisions and supplies for their army. (During this period, England did not have a standing army. The fighting was done by volunteers.)

In the case of the Parliamentary army, the brunt of the fighting in the first part of the Civil War was done by men who had been locally recruited and trained. Their primary interest was to serve near their homes. They were poorly clothed, poorly supplied, poorly fed and poorly paid. Desertions ran high. Cromwell realized that he must do something quickly or lose the war. He decided to resort to conscription. Parliament would assume the responsibility of training the army and providing for its support.

Cromwell had wisely realized that a new start

was necessary. It was a decision that eventually determined the outcome of the war. He said, "Let us apply ourselves to the remedy. Let us put the army onto a new path." The result was the New Model Army. It would be inspired by the vision, energy, and zeal of Oliver Cromwell and those he trained.

Cromwell's vision and that of his followers was the rightness of their cause in the service of God. Historian Thomas Carlyle states that "no one can ever be so sure again as Cromwell that God was on his side." Indeed, Cromwell was convinced of that. He encouraged that belief in his men and it worked. It worked superbly. His was an age when religion and life were inseparable, so no matter on which side a man fought, and whether he professed godliness or not, few in the ranks doubted that God ruled the world and that His will would prevail.

Sermons, prayers, and psalm singing were as regular a part of garrison routine as training in the field. Two sermons were preached to the troops every Sabbath and another on Thursday. There was the reading of a chapter of Scripture each morning before the placing of the guards. There has never been another army like it. This, then, was the army that Bunyan went off to join.

Ola Elizabeth Winslow holds that "there is little evidence that Bunyan would have satisfied Cromwell's hope for the ideal soldier—a soldier who knew what he fought for and who loved the cause. Bunyan may have been indifferent to the preaching and arguing about religion which went on about him, but he could not have escaped incessant exposure to it."

There can be no doubt that Bunyan heard many religious discussions during his time in the army. The popular name for the New Model Army was "The People's Army." It was made up of a cross section of society. It also included a variety of Protestant religious affiliations. Winslow notes: "On the extreme right were the Presbyterians and the ex-Royalists; in the middle, the conservative Dissenters or Congregationalists; and on the extreme left, the Levellers, Baptists, and Fifth Monarchists."

In civilian society, among the Puritan groups on the left of the religious spectrum were the Independents. The Independents wanted to form churches composed of only those who could demonstrate the fruits of personal salvation. They felt that it was imperative for them to separate themselves from the state church. This decision made them very unpopular with the religious authorities. It was to this Independent tradition that Bunyan would, after his conversion, belong.

Bunyan describes his brief military career in less than ninety words. Some believe that he saw no action whatsoever. Others assert that he probably saw action during small forays against Royalist strongholds in the neighborhood. These local engagements usually involved fifty or less men and lasted no more than several hours. Soldiers ordinarily took turns on such missions, usually as volunteers. In his autobiography, Bunyan relates how a man who had swapped duties with him was killed one dark night by a musket ball through his head. There, but for the grace of God, would have gone John Bunyan. At the time Bunyan may well have believed that he was simply lucky and the other man unlucky. In later years, however, he would see the event as one of many providences of God in his life.

In his book *Cromwell's Army*, Sir Charles Firth mentions how that army abounded with visionaries. He contends that nearly every leader and many a soldier was also a preacher and a theologian. "At first, the New Model Army tried to prevent unlicensed preaching. They found it impossible to do so. The soldiers believed strongly that they were fighting for both freedom of religion and freedom of speech." Battles opened and closed with prayer. It was perhaps only natural that Puritan sentiments and ideals so dominated Parliament's army. Roger Sharrock declares that "the mass of Puritans led a life of disciplined moral effort directed toward the discovery of some assurance of their salvation. Their effort was to produce a holy community, established to do spiritual battle." To them, the Civil War was in some ways a visible outworking of spiritual conflicts.

There can be no doubt that during his brief

army duty Bunyan heard many sermons on the subject of the return of the Lord. Feeling was strong in the Puritan army that the Lord's return was near. Bunyan no doubt received (as nearly all the conscripts did) a copy of the "Soldier's Pocket Bible." Perhaps he read it, perhaps he didn't. Perhaps only a seed was planted, for his outward life changed little. He was discharged from the army and returned home as—in his own words—"a sin-breeder and a brisk talker." God had not yet begun his deepest dealings with John Bunyan.

John Bunyan had thus survived the Civil War untouched either by enemy bullets or the stern morality of the Puritan message. There was, however, another force at work in his life, a force that would have an immediate impact upon him. Although the facts are lost to history, John Bunyan had somehow made the acquaintance of a young woman during his army days. History does not even record her name, although most of Bunyan's biographers believe that it was Mary. This conjecture is based mostly upon the fact that their first daughter was named Mary, just as their first son was named John. Although Bunyan himself makes mention of neither his wife's name nor the names of his children in his autobiography, *Grace Abounding*, Gwilym O. Griffith reports: "It is plain that the beginning of Bunyan's reformation dates back to his courtship and marriage, which we may put somewhere about 1647–1649."

At any rate, his heart began to draw him home once again to Elstow. The time he had spent in the army had to a large degree healed any estrangement that existed between his father and himself. His top priority now was to work with his father and thus fulfill his years of apprenticeship in his chosen profession. John, like his father before him, would be a tinker. Marriage began to be the predominating theme in his mind. But in order to marry his sweetheart, he first had to establish himself in business and find a home. He had to find or fashion the tools of his trade in order to be able to make a living and support his wife. He and a friend forged the heavy anvil (which still exists today among the Bunyan memorabilia) which he would need.

Vera Brittain describes John Bunyan during the period between his demobilization and his marriage in this way: "He seemed to his friends to be a strong, cheerful young man of enormous energy, with no problems more complex than that of earning a living. He gave himself up for a time to pursuits which attracted his natural high spirits. He joined in various sports—wrestling, jumping, pitching the bar, ninepins, and dancing. At that time the thoughts and practices of religion were tedious to him." He said of this period in his life: "I could not endure religion myself, nor that anyone else should." Once he had finally gone into business for himself, he found a small cottage with a thatched roof in

Elstow. He decided to marry Mary without further delay. Tools he had, but furniture he had not. It was clearly a love match. Bunyan described their condition in this way: "We came together as poor as poor might be, not having so much household stuff as a dish or spoon betwixt us both."

Bunyan's wife brought no dowry except for two books: *The Plain Man's Pathway to Heaven* and *The Practice of Piety*. Books were rare and precious in those days. It is to be assumed, in fact, that the Bunyans felt themselves indeed blessed to have them. Monica Furlong writes that "although intensely tedious by modern standards, these books were avidly, almost reverently read by the couple, Bunyan probably reading aloud to his wife." She also apparently brought a godly heritage to their union. Bunyan wrote that "my mercy was to light upon a wife whose father was counted godly." His wife clearly had a beneficial impact on Bunyan. The books that she brought into their home and the many conversations they had about godly things (including what she had learned of the Lord at her father's knee) slowly began to touch John's heart. He said that her books did indeed "beget within me some desire to religion." It appears that he was especially affected by the description in *The Practice of Piety* of the misery of people who face death without being reconciled to Christ. He began to attend church and "both said and sang as others did."

One day the sermon seemed to pierce his heart, a heart that he was well aware had remained hard and cold in the midst of his new orientation. Feeling that the sermon applied perfectly to him, he returned home quite shaken. As is often the case, however, this good word did not take root in his heart. Stirred and troubled by it at first, he "forgot about it after a good meal." At this point, Bunyan's conformity to God's Word was strictly external. He thus "shook the sermon out of mind" and returned to the village green. His greatest delights were games and sports. Up to that point it had never occurred to him that his newfound interest and attachment to religion should affect the way he led his life. He little realized that God would confront him for the second time that day there on the village green in a most dramatic way.

Bunyan joined his companions for a game of "cat." In this game a player knocks a small piece of wood from the ground with a bat. Once the cat is airborne, the player then hits it as far as he can with his bat. On this particular day, John had knocked the cat into the air and was set to give it a second blow when he was frozen in his tracks by a voice both majestic and threatening. The voice pierced Bunyan's heart with this question: "Wilt thou leave thy sins and go to heaven; or have thy sins and go to hell?"

At that time John Bunyan was still captive to the stern, Old Testament approach of most of the

Puritan preachers that he had encountered throughout his life, both in Elstow and in the army. Brittain remarks that "his mind was still captive, his spirit not yet free. Only with great suffering would the meaning of the Cross later come to him with its message of love and forgiveness." At that moment, however, it seemed to him that all hope of heaven was gone for good. For the next month he gave himself over to the dictates of his fleshly nature, reasoning, as many have done, that if he could never gain heaven, he might as well perfect the art of sinning. But once again, he got a course rectification from an unexpected source.

John had a proclivity (and some say a facility) for swearing. He had to some degree perfected his swearing during his days in the army. Once he had decided to "continue in sin with greediness of mind," it was inevitable that old habits, only recently and minimally affected by his temporary interest in spiritual things, would return with an even greater force. He stood one day before a local shop window "belching out oaths." The owner of the shop was a woman with a notorious reputation as an evildoer. All the same, she strongly rebuked Bunyan for his swearing. Her reproof struck him like lightning and thunder. He wished mightily that he could somehow begin again, although he despaired of being able to change himself. Somehow, however, his swearing began to lessen and eventually ceased. Brittain describes the experience this way: "Unaware as he was still of its true significance, the Voice that he had heard on the village green had heralded the moment of spiritual birth. Like the Voice heard by Saul on the road to Damascus, it called him to leave the old careless, lascivious ways. It summoned him to a hard life of self-discipline and service, where persecution and imprisonment were privileges, and death was the great reward."

Soundly shaken, Bunyan began to consider his fate. He struggled for a month or more with the choice he felt he had been given—without any victory. He then met a poor man who spoke to him of the Bible in such glowing and endearing terms that he felt himself stirred to read it. He began to read the Bible for himself for the first time. He especially enjoyed the historical books and he made his best efforts to obey the Ten Commandments. He came eventually to feel rather pleased with his spiritual progress. He saw himself as reformed and thought that he "pleased God as well as any man in England," later recording that his neighbors "did marvel much to see such a great and famous alteration in my life and manners." Although the process of his becoming what might be considered a "religious man" had begun, he would later write of his spiritual condition then that he "knew not Christ, nor grace, nor faith, nor hope."

As many (or perhaps most) have done, Bunyan sought to make himself acceptable to God through his actions. In his heart, though, he knew that he was still far from God, and at that time was still unaware of how he might narrow that gap. He decided that perhaps he needed to give up some of his simple pleasures, hoping that this sacrificial gesture would earn him God's favor. In his autobiography, he tells how he gave up ringing the church bells at Elstow simply because it gave him too much pleasure. He contented himself with only watching and listening to them as they were rung. Eventually, he forsook even that small pleasure.

Bell ringing would certainly not seem to be much of a vice to us. The historical truth, however, is that church bell ringers were usually a rowdy group. They generally did not attend church services and often drank heavily, at work and elsewhere. Bunyan, who during that time in his life was drawn naturally to merriment, perhaps made a wise decision when he decided to distance himself from bell ringing and bell ringers. He likewise had to struggle long and hard against his enjoyment of dancing, but eventually felt constrained to renounce that too. Alas, it was all to no avail.

It was during this period of good works and outward conformity that a daughter was born to John and Mary Bunyan. She was christened on July 20, 1650. History does not record when her parents first realized, and then accepted, that she had been born blind. It does record, however, that John Bunyan was a kind and affectionate husband and father. He dearly loved his wife and daughter.

4

Chapter Four

John Gifford and Bedford

Among the Puritans, conversion was not generally the result of a sudden upheaval. The entire process might be spread out over a number of years. Bunyan once described salvation as "a work of many steps." Biographer Roger Sharrock explains that "conversion was to result in the sanctification of all mental and practical activities of the convert." This ongoing process deepened and expanded as it went, touching and filling both the mind and the heart.

Bunyan, however, although heavily influenced by Puritanism, did not yet understand the Word of God. He had not yet grasped that man can never justify himself before a holy God. He did not understand the working of grace. There is a line of poetry that goes: "In a dark time the eye begins to see." That was true in Bunyan's case. Feeling himself to be on the trail of God, he did not yet realize that actually it was God who was on his trail. Scripture is quite clear that in the process that leads to salvation it is God who is the originator, not man.

One of God's favorite methods for reaching people is to use other people. This was the case with John Bunyan. As often occurs in His working to win the hearts of men and women, God also uses circumstances. Frank Mott Harrison writes that "man is wont to blame his occupation for hindering his spiritual life. And such may sometimes be the case. But God can use the means of livelihood in saving a perishing soul. It was so with John Bunyan. The employment he could get at Elstow was not enough to support a wife and child; and that a blind one. So he had to seek work in Bedford-town, a mile or so away."

Bedford was the home of Pastor John Gifford—a remarkable man. Biographer Gwilym O. Griffith believes that Gifford was probably the only true man of genius that Bunyan knew in his formational years. Gifford had fought in the Civil War as an officer on the Royalist side. With the defeat of Charles I, Gifford was thrown into prison, awaiting execution. He escaped, took shelter in Bedford, and began to practice medicine. In those days, he was recognized as a swashbuckling sort—given to drinking and gambling. In some way or other, however, he came across "a Puritan book." He read it and was "mightily laid hold upon" and powerfully converted. Eventually he became part of a small group of twelve Dissenters. Dissenters were those who supported the Puritan theology in opposition to the state church. He immediately showed a great gift for preaching, leadership and teaching and soon became their pastor. Together, this sturdy little group formed the Bedford church in 1650.

It became common during this period for laymen to found independent Puritan congregations. The Baptist denomination grew out of this religious movement. The first Baptist church on English soil had been established in 1612, just outside London. Although the Bedford church was an independent Baptist church, it was Calvinist in doctrine. As Baptists, its members believed in adult believers' baptism, although they did not insist upon it as a requirement for membership. Although Pastor Gifford would die only five years later, he was to play a pivotal role in John Bunyan's life.

About this time, Bunyan went to Bedford to seek work. It proved to be a providential day for him. While there, he overheard a discussion among "four old women sitting in the sun." They spoke glowingly yet naturally of the grace of God and the experience of the new birth. Bunyan realized that despite his good works, he was not saved—that he was "but a poor painted hypocrite." In *Grace Abounding,* Bunyan described his meeting with these simple women: "Thus, when I had heard and considered what they said, I left them and went about my employment again, but their talk and conversation went with me, while my heart remained with them."

Bunyan states that these women were "far

above, out of my reach. They talked of God visiting their souls with His love in the Lord Jesus." He heard these simple and sincere women "condemn, slight, and abhor their own righteousness as filthy and insufficient to do them any good." He recounts that his heart began to shake within him as he realized that he must be born again. These women were members of John Gifford's church. "They spake as if joy did make them speak." Then and there Bunyan began to attach himself to these humble and joy-filled people, feeling drawn to them, returning often to fellowship with a widening circle of new friends.

Bunyan would later on have an almost prophetic dream based on his experience of conversing with this band of holy and joyful women. He dreamed about the people of Bedford. In his dream, these godly people dwelt happily together, warm and secure on the sunny side of a mountain, while he was alone on the other side, trapped in frost and snow. He searched and searched for a way to reach them until he found a small passage which he was eventually able to squeeze through. That tight gap through which he could barely squeeze was, he concluded, the narrow gate mentioned in Matthew 7:13. Clearly, his heart yearned to place itself under the life-giving warmth of the Sun of Righteousness.

It was only natural that his new friends would introduce him to John Gifford. Mr. Sharrock writes: "Gifford may have recognized a kindred spirit in Bunyan, another strong and passionate nature which had to undergo division before it could be reconciled with itself. He thought well of Bunyan from the start and invited him to his house to hear others giving an account of their spiritual experiences." In time, Bunyan would tell of his spiritual journey to others in the church at Bedford. For the time being, his calling was to listen. He enjoyed hearing Gifford "conferring with others about the dealings of their souls." Under the tender guidance of Gifford and his friends, Bunyan began to read the Bible "with new eyes." He began to seriously study the epistles of Paul, repositories of the theology of grace and election.

John visited Pastor Gifford often. Sometimes they sat in his study and spoke together. Other times they walked and talked in his garden. Monica Furlong has written that Bunyan always "spoke of Mr. Gifford with great respect, as of a kindly father, and with the finding of this father he described himself as being 'led from truth to truth.'" Bunyan himself said that Gifford's words "came upon me as rain and were much for my stability."

Gradually, Bunyan's concept of a God of Wrath gave way to an understanding of Him as a God of Reconciliation. As that revelation grew, his fears were slowly replaced with hope and assurance. This growing confidence clearly called for a specific commitment, so Bunyan was baptized by Gifford one starry night in a local river inlet. Ms. Brittain writes that "the quiet solemnity of his midnight baptism made him feel that a divine power, profound, mysterious, and never again to be denied, had at last taken charge of his tempestuous life." John thus joined Gifford's church in 1653 (at the midpoint of his quest for assurance), throwing his lot in with the Puritans, abandoning the more formal and ritualistic church in Elstow.

In 1654, the Bunyans had a second daughter, Elizabeth. In 1655 he moved his family to Bedford to be closer to the church which had become the center of his life.

The years between 1651 and 1655 were years of both elation and torment for Bunyan. This intense struggle is recorded in his autobiography, *Grace Abounding to the Chief of Sinners.* The story of his long struggle toward a clear assurance of salvation is unsurpassed in the whole of literature. It is highly reminiscent in some ways of Job's epic struggle. Monica Furlong remarks that it is the story of a man "wrestling furiously with his God in an attempt to grasp the riddle of man's existence. He charted this fearful period of his life with minute precision. Step by step, God was building His truth into John Bunyan's life, drawing him into an assurance of his salvation, preparing him for his life's work."

Chapter Five

5

John Bunyan and Assurance

It is difficult for many people in this current age of "easy believism" and "cheap grace" to understand the intense soul searching John Bunyan went through as he pursued an assurance of his salvation. Just as we are products of the age in which we live, Bunyan was a product of his own age. Why was an assurance of salvation so important to him? In order to answer that question, we must understand a little bit about what the Puritans believed. They were strict Calvinists. Calvinist doctrine—both then and now—stresses God's sovereignty. Calvinists believe that God chooses those who will be saved: all who are saved have been sovereignly elected to salvation. It was this doctrine of election that spurred John Bunyan to an almost frantic search in God's Word for the assurance of *his* salvation. Although God's election was believed to be unconditional and irresistible, it was still up to the individual Puritan believer to seek God until he came into a final *assurance* of salvation upon which he could establish his faith. Since this assurance was of the greatest importance, Calvinists at times tended to be intensely introspective. Bunyan "perfected" this introspection to a high art form. Henri A. Talon wrote that Bunyan recorded his spiritual struggles in *Grace Abounding* "to serve his faith and help his fellows." The two primary strains of thought in this book are, accordingly, self-examination and evangelism.

Calvinist theology of that day more or less outlined a spiritual journey. The first step in this journey is, from the human standpoint, conviction of sin. After that comes God's calling, the evidence of election (also called assurance of salvation), justification by faith, sanctification (a clear and apparent growth in holiness of life), and finally, glorification. Glorification is the end of the pilgrim's spiritual journey—an end reached only in heaven. The key to this journey is the fact of election. This doctrine was the reason for Bunyan's deep introspections and his ongoing search for God's will in a study of His Word.

"It may be said that he, of all Englishmen of his time, or of any other time, stands out as the man with the Book in his hands," states Gwilym O. Griffith. Bunyan's search for personal assurance of salvation eventually led him to become one of the best-versed Bible teachers of his time. Ironically, however, for a season the Bible seemed to him a source of both terror and consolation. Scriptures chased each other through his mind, alternately condemning and exonerating him.

Calvinists, it has been said, are caught in the "Catch-22" position of being quite unsure if they are actually among the elect of God while at the same time seeking to live as though they are.

Motivated as he was to gain an assurance of his salvation, Bunyan hopefully and eagerly listened to the testimonies of those at the Bedford church who had gained the assurance he was seeking. It was then customary for those who had gained this assurance to share publicly the story of their trials, temptations, and eventual victory. The testimonies of his friends and the preaching of John Gifford were a definite encouragement to him. While Gifford's sharing, friendship, counseling and preaching made a great impact on Bunyan, the turning point in his early quest came from a different but equally God-inspired direction.

John Bunyan had begun to wish that he might be able to study "the experience of some ancient godly man, from whose temptations he might learn wisdom." He felt that God guided him to a bookshop. There in a pile of old books he found a copy of Martin Luther's *Commentary on the Epistle of St. Paul to the Galatians.* It was an impressive and imposing work: 542 pages of verse-by-verse commentary on Galatians. It seemed to Bunyan that Luther's book had been written directly to him. Luther's own life had been revolutionized when he read about justification by faith in Christ, and his commentary on this portion of

God's Word had a similar effect on John. It was as if scales fell from his eyes. He wrote: "I found my condition largely and profoundly handled, as if his book had been written out of my heart." It was then that he realized that he had been putting himself under the Law, trying to establish a righteousness of his own, a righteousness that was not according to faith. Bunyan had finally begun to understand the grace of God. He commented: "I was finally able to look from myself to Christ."

Gwilym O. Griffith states that "Luther's book taught him that the secret of his peace (assurance) lay not in his own heart, but in the heart of God." He finally understood that "righteousness was nowhere to be found but in the Person of Jesus Christ." Frank Mott Harrison adds that "John Bunyan had firmly grasped the eternal truth—that only the Blood of Christ can remove the guilt of sin, sin that was to him both real and terrible." Bunyan himself states that Luther's book above all others (excepting the Bible) was "fit for a wounded conscience."

Bunyan's faith had truly taken root. In the Kingdom of God—as elsewhere—root always precedes fruit. Yet, though he was energized in a greater way than ever before, there would still be further intense struggles for him before he would finally come into a place of permanent rest in Christ. Depending on his frame of mind, he would find that portions of Scripture either lifted him up or condemned him. He would relate in turn to Bible heroes and to Bible villains, thereupon feeling either relieved or condemned by his conscience. As many people do, he even struggled for a season with the idea that perhaps he had committed the unpardonable sin. But truth progressively won out. His struggles enabled him to grow stronger in his faith, a degree at a time. With each breakthrough, his faith increased. Bunyan described a key experience in this way: "But one day as I was passing in the field, and that too with some dashes on my conscience, fearing lest all was not right, suddenly this sentence fell upon my soul, 'Thy righteousness is in heaven.' " It set him free. He would later write, "I thought I could have spoken of His love, and of His mercy to me, even to the very crows that sat upon the plowed lands before me."

Chapter Six

Bunyan the Preacher

There are no self-made men in the Kingdom of God. In fact, quite the opposite is true. In order to be called into service by the Lord, we must be willing to die to ourselves (a strange concept in this age of self-esteem). He is the potter; we are the clay. John Bunyan understood quite well the truth he found in John 15:16. He understood that he had not chosen *God* but that God had chosen *him*. He also understood, through the revelation of God's Word, that he was called to bear fruit for God.

Clearly, God gives to all believers gifts and talents that can be perfected in His service: gifts and talents that will please Him and bring Him glory. Bunyan's long period of retrospective self-analysis in the light of God's Word had a dual effect (a very beneficial effect) on him. It caused him to lose faith in his flesh—in the natural man. It also created in him a hunger to know God personally through a deep and ongoing study of His Word, and then to serve Him. It was this continual study of God's Word—the day-by-day hiding of it in his heart (Ps. 119:11)—that eventually enabled him to become the evangelist and writer God had ordained he would be. It also put the steel in his heart that he would need in order to stand in the hard times that eventually come to us all.

When John Bunyan joined the Bedford Baptist church in 1653 he was listed on the church roll as the twenty-sixth member. When he moved his family to Bedford in 1655 he had no way of knowing that he would shortly be required to endure two devastating losses. For it was in that year that his friend and mentor John Gifford died. Gifford had been a faithful friend as well as a spiritual father to John Bunyan. On his deathbed, Pastor Gifford urged his flock to love one another and to stand firm. Soon afterward, Bunyan would also lose his dear wife.

How then did John Bunyan the tinker become John Bunyan the preacher? Ola Elizabeth Winslow tells us that "Bunyan possessed in generous measure the peculiar gifts of eloquence and personal magnetism that mark an evangelist in any age. It would seem that the brethren of the congregation recognized his gift of public speaking before he himself knew that he possessed it." John Gifford had already been using him as a visitor to members of the Bedford church in their homes. Probably Bunyan's first opportunity to speak before a group (he describes himself as "excessively shy" in those early days) was when he gave his testimony before a selected group of church members in a meeting supervised by Gifford. He was also, no doubt, obliged to give his testimony publicly as a requirement for joining the Bedford church. Winslow adds that "occasionally Bunyan spoke a word of exhortation at the church meetings and at several 'private assemblies' where he later admitted that others were 'affected and comforted.'" Vera Brittain asserts that "now the father of a third child, he had made rapid progress in the congregation which he had recently joined with so deep a sense of unworthiness. He had been a member for about two years when a request by his fellow-members to say a word at one of their gatherings led to the discovery of a gift for preaching which surprised both himself and them. Soon he was invited to accompany the brethren on expeditions into the country, where the words that he added to their homilies showed that his eloquence could be relied on."

There were two factors in Bunyan's life that motivated him toward preaching. He himself records that "some of the most able among the saints" in Bedford urged him to begin preaching. He initially found the prospect of preaching quite daunting, because he was still struggling to apprehend the peace of God that was to accompany his assurance of salvation. His second (and most important) impetus to preach came from "a pricking forward in his mind," an awareness that it would displease the Holy Spirit if he chose to bury the gifts the Lord had given him in order to be fruitful in service. He did not hurry into this new calling, however, but started with a season of fervent prayer, fasting, and some trial efforts.

John Bunyan's ministry as a preacher had its start sometime in the year 1656. This was fifteen years before his call and ordination as Bedford Baptist's pastor in 1671. The person who in January 1656 succeeded John Gifford as pastor of the Bedford church was a young man named John Burton—not to be confused with John Bunyan. Bunyan was still just a member of the church.

After he had mastered speaking within his own church, Bunyan began to speak to small groups of people who met in private homes, barns, or even outdoors. This continued for two years or more, and his reputation as a preacher (as well as his ability to preach) grew. His apparent success was a reassurance to him. He later wrote that "once I set upon the work, people came to hear the Word by hundreds, and that from all parts." Nobody was more surprised than Bunyan himself. Finally convinced that he was indeed called to preach God's Word, he went forth with the blessing of his church.

Among his first truly public outings, Bunyan publicly opposed the heretical teaching of the Quakers in the Bedford area in open-air debates. The Quakers of John Bunyan's time were not like the peace-loving Quakers of our day. In those days, the Quakers were very militant about their beliefs, going as far as disrupting church services to make their views known, shouting down those who opposed their views. They believed that their "inner leading" superseded the authority of the written Scriptures. This was a belief that John Bunyan could not leave unopposed. He saw Quaker doctrine as tantamount to contempt for the Word of God. This burden also led to Bunyan's first published work, a refutation of the Quaker position.

At the outset of his preaching career Bunyan "at first could not believe that God should speak by him to the heart of any man." Each opportunity to preach was an emotional one for him. He says that at times he felt as if his legs would not support him as he mounted the pulpit stairs. For the first two years, his preaching was primarily "a crying out against men's sins." A contemporary described the fiery young preacher as "of a stern and rough temper which did strike something of awe in them that had nothing of the fear of God in them." He says that he preached what he "smartingly did feel." John avers that in those early days he "went as if in chains to preach to them in chains, and carried that fire in my own conscience that I persuaded them to beware of."

While it was not then unusual for a man such as Bunyan (a man who was self-taught in the Scriptures rather than university educated) to preach the gospel in rural England, it was also not unusual that he would be held in less than high esteem in some quarters. A famed university scholar demanded of him on one occasion what right he had to expound upon the Scriptures when he was unable to read the Scriptures in the original languages. Bunyan, not learned but wise, asked him if he had the original manuscripts in his personal possession. The man of course said that he did not, but that he had access to what he believed to be true copies. Bunyan replied, "And I believe the English Bible to be a true copy also." God was his defense and his justification. On one occasion, a noted Cambridge scholar came "to hear the tinker prate." During the sermon, however, he was so profoundly touched by God that for a long time afterwards he would listen to nobody other than John Bunyan.

The great Puritan vice-chancellor of Oxford University, John Owen, often went to hear John Bunyan preach. He was once asked by Charles II why he went so frequently to hear Bunyan speak. Owen replied that he would gladly exchange all of his learning for the ability to preach as the Tinker of Bedford did. By that time Bunyan's preaching had matured, nourished by study and revelation, by the words of faith and sound doctrine. Bunyan described it in this way: "God let me into something of the mystery of union with Christ, wherefore I discovered and showed it to them also."

Biographer Roger Sharrock has written that "Bunyan emerged from the years of despair preceding his conversion a new man: his faith released him from morbid introspection: the massive strength of his mind which had been divided against itself was now integrated and applied, efficiently and courageously, to the affairs of the Bedford separatist church." It had become clear to all that Bunyan had grown greatly in the grace of the Lord. His evangelistic preaching was becoming ever more powerful, and the door to fruitful service in the Lord seemed wide open to him. In addition, he and Mary had been blessed by the birth of their fourth child, Thomas. Bunyan was unprepared for the sudden death of his beloved wife in 1658. Although she has remained a shadowy figure in history, what shines through most clearly about her in the writings of John Bunyan is the love that they shared. Vera Brittain writes that "Mary thus died, a frail young woman prematurely exhausted by ten years of marriage." Bunyan was left alone to raise four young children under the age of ten.

7
Chapter Seven

Remarriage

As Bunyan's preaching skills grew, his reputation likewise burgeoned. He faithfully told his listeners about the atonement of Christ. He later wrote, "I did much labor to hold forth Jesus Christ in all His Offices, Relations, and Benefits unto the world." In *Grace Abounding* he said that he "came to understand that it was through the blood shed on Mount Calvary that He did save and redeem sinners as clearly and as really with the eyes of my soul as ever methought I had seen a penny loaf bought with a penny." Assured of his own salvation, he ministered that hope to others. It was a message that people wanted and needed. His sermons are said to have been "lucid, virile, humorous, and direct." Vera Brittain has described him as "the type of preacher whose vigor and inspiration are a speaking rebuke to professional conventionality." In short, he was a plain-spoken man who was faithful to the message of Scripture.

As his reputation expanded, he came increasingly under the scrutiny of local officials. Bunyan knew quite well that it was inevitable that he would eventually be arrested because of his public witness. It was the knowledge that he could be imprisoned at any time that caused him to do some serious reflection and soul-searching. Realizing that he might have to leave all for the sake of his conscience and convictions, he felt compelled to make arrangements for the support of his family. Biographer Frank Mott Harrison informs us that "he besought his God to guide him, and the answer was clear—marry." So in 1659 he married a young woman who was, probably, a member of the Bedford church. Her name was Elizabeth. Ola Elizabeth Winslow observes that "although we know little of her background, in Bunyan's later life we will know her for her courage, her resourcefulness and independence." Some biographers believe that Elizabeth had been a friend of Mary Bunyan. Quite possibly she was one of the group of women who were helping take care of John Bunyan's children after the death of his wife. It seems clear that Bunyan was exceptionally fortunate in *both* of his wives.

Elizabeth's courage, responsibility, and loyalty would be a tremendous encouragement to her husband in the coming years. She would also enable him to fulfill his calling.

Chapter Eight

Arrest!

When Charles II returned from abroad to be crowned King in 1660, the Puritan era was for all practical purposes over. The spiritual edifice that the Puritans had raised up was immediately dismantled. In its place, the state church established its own religious system. Henceforth, preachers would have to be licensed by the state. This move came as a terrible blow to the Puritans, who believed that unlicensed and unlettered men like John Bunyan were rightly preaching God's pure Word. Sermons were the foundation stone of Puritan worship. They believed that in most cases preaching was the key that opened the door to salvation for people.

The area around Bedford had not had a bishop for nearly two decades. When Robert Sanderson, the new bishop, entered Bedford on October 17, 1660, it was to the sound of repeated volleys of musket-fire and loud shouts of welcome. Bunyan heard the sounds of the celebration from his prison cell.

About one month earlier, John Bunyan had

made his way from his home in Bedford to the hamlet of Lower Samsell, about thirteen miles away. He had often in the past preached to a gathering there and that night he had an opportunity to preach there again. It was a remote and somewhat secluded place. A large hawthorn tree grew near the house, and he had frequently preached under it during summer months. The Puritans who gathered secretly for meetings like this knew they had to be careful, for it was clearly against the decrees of the new state church. They were under orders to attend the local parish church and to forsake meetings such as this one. John Bunyan was not a licensed preacher, of course.

Upon entering the house that night, Bunyan immediately noticed the tense attitude among the people gathered there. The house owner took him aside and warned him that a warrant had been issued for his arrest—a warrant that would be served the very next time he preached "outside the law." Bunyan was unmoved and encouraged them not to be afraid. Nevertheless, he went outside, taking the opportunity to seek God in prayer. He had good reasons to be cautious. For one thing, Elizabeth was now pregnant. He made up his mind, however, that his cause was just. He later declared: "I was resolved to see the utmost of what they could say or do unto me: for, blessed be the Lord, I knew of no evil that I had said or done." He returned inside to begin the meeting.

Bunyan, of course, was already somewhat of a marked man. His preaching had gained him a reputation in the Bedford area. As far as he was concerned, politics mattered but little. His main interest was to deliver "an awakening word." Although he tried to avoid controversy, many of the pro-Royalist gentry around Bedford regarded his preaching as inflammatory. They felt that his Puritan style and content were fanning the flames of discontent toward the restored regime and the state church. Bunyan refused to yield to fear, holding fast to his calling. He knew he must preach what he believed to be the truth, to those who needed to hear the message—no matter what the consequences might be.

Bunyan had hardly begun to preach that evening when the constable was at the door, warrant in hand. The constable made a quick search and was confused and disconcerted to find no weapon more dangerous to the state than the Sword of the Spirit. After he had calmed and encouraged them, Bunyan bid his small group of friends farewell, encouraging them to remain true and reminding them that it was both a calling and an honor to suffer thus for the sake of Christ and His gospel.

Bunyan was marched to the home of Francis Wingate, the local magistrate, who lived about a mile away. He was released into the care of a local farmer because Wingate was not at home. The next morning Bunyan returned to the home of

Mr. Wingate to face the charges against him. The magistrate believed that such gatherings were bound to be more political than religious in nature since he knew many people throughout the land were not happy with the return of Charles II and with what they considered to be religious oppression. Wingate was, therefore, surprised to hear that no firearms had been found in the meeting.

The specific charge against John Bunyan was violation of the Conventicle Act of 1593, promulgated under the reign of Elizabeth I. This act stipulated that any person who went to worship anywhere outside the parish church should be imprisoned for three months. If after the three months he refused to repent, he could then be subject to either exile or execution. The law had fallen into disuse, but it was still on the books—the perfect tool to snare a well-known preacher like John Bunyan.

Bunyan refused to yield an inch under Wingate's accusations, insults and questions, defending himself most capably. He steadfastly refused to promise that he would no longer preach the Word of God. Wingate was joined in his questioning by a local vicar, Dr. Lindall, who treated the "uneducated" Bunyan with scorn. The debate became heated for a moment as Bunyan answered accusations with passages of Scripture. Lindall was later replaced in the questioning by William Foster, the Bedford Justice of the Peace and self-appointed legal champion of orthodox religion. He also was unable to sway Bunyan. Through it all, Bunyan clung stubbornly to his position that God's children have the right to worship God as they see fit.

Taking his stand on Scripture, Bunyan answered his captors with dignity and wisdom. Unable to shake him, they gave Bunyan a final choice. He must renounce preaching or go to prison. Bunyan chose the latter, simply informing them that if they were to release him today, he would again be preaching tomorrow. His fate was sealed. Off he went to the County Gaol,* "with God's comfort in his poor soul." In happier times, Bunyan and other members of the Bedford congregation had visited prisoners in the Bedford Gaol. Now Bunyan would be a prisoner and his friends would visit *him* there.

* This is simply the British spelling of the word "jail."

Chapter Nine

Trial

The news that John Bunyan had been arrested quickly spread throughout the area. Undeterred, Bunyan saw himself as a prisoner of the Lord and was resolved to find God's will for his life in this new and difficult situation. The County Gaol in Bedford was a building with two floors. The ground floor was used for felons; the top floor was primarily for debtors. The jail had neither infirmary nor bathing facilities. The prisoners slept on straw and usually suffered greatly from the cold. This facility was more of a detention center than it was a prison for hardened criminals—who were usually either hanged or flogged and released. So the Bedford County Gaol housed mostly debtors, political prisoners, or people who (like Bunyan) were awaiting trial for a variety of offenses. Circumstances often tended to produce overcrowding, and overcrowding could lead in turn to starvation and disease. Corruption prevailed, and families of wealthy prisoners could buy privileges for their loved ones. Poverty-stricken prisoners might rot away in prison for years, neglected and for all practical purposes forgotten.

It was into this world that John Bunyan went on the fourteenth of November in the year 1660. He remained imprisoned for seven weeks, awaiting his summons for a preliminary hearing—a hearing which came in January 1661. So far as money was concerned, Bunyan could probably have had bail arranged for him by members of the Bedford church. However, he was not eligible for bail because he had refused to give the authorities his word that he would not resume his preaching. It was a difficult time for John and his family. Of it, he wrote, "I saw in this condition I was a man who was pulling down his house upon the head of his wife and children: yet thought I, I must do it, I must do it." His wife Elizabeth went into labor prematurely, and after an agonizing week she lost the baby. When she had sufficiently recovered, she visited her husband, accompanied by his daughter Mary, as often as she could.

The charges against Bunyan were that he "devilishly and perniciously abstained from coming to church" and that he was holding illegal meetings at which he preached. Bunyan answered to the charges that he indeed did attend church but not the *parish* church. When asked why not, he responded that it was not so commanded in God's Word. In the discussion that followed, Bunyan explained also that he was not commanded by Scripture to use the *Book of Com-*

mon Prayer in his worship. It seems strange to modern readers that a court of law might prosecute a man along theological lines, but Bunyan lived in an age of theological ferment.

Bunyan more than held his own as he was thoroughly questioned by the learned prosecutors. Somewhat like the apostle Paul at his court appearance, Bunyan felt himself inspired and quickened by the Holy Spirit. He defended himself strictly with the Scriptures that he so loved and which he had so diligently studied. His eloquent defense both confounded and enraged his interrogators. In the end, however, Bunyan was forced to admit that he was guilty of breaking the King's laws (although he clearly demonstrated to the magistrates that he felt he was simply obeying the True King). In the end, the prosecutors got what they wanted. Bunyan said, "I confess we have had many meetings together, both to pray to God and to exhort one another, and there we had the sweet comforting presence of the Lord among us for our encouragement." In anger and frustration, the authorities remanded him once again into the custody of his jailers, there to remain for another three months. They put him under the threat of banishment if after three months he still refused to comply with the royal decree. Later, Bunyan wrote that his heart "was truly refreshed in the time of [his] examination, and afterwards at returning to prison."

Bunyan was well aware what his incarceration would cost him and his family. He said that being separated from them was "like having [his] flesh torn from [his] bones." He was especially concerned over the fate of his blind daughter, Mary. Determined to accept his situation and resolved to trust God come what may, he asked that his wife bring him his Bible and his concordance. In the long, hard days to come, they would bring him much comfort and encouragement. They would also aid him in serving God in the way for which he is now known best—as a writer.

Because he had been arrested under an obscure law that dated back to the time of Elizabeth I, at the beginning Bunyan had hopes that justice and common sense would prevail. When he realized that powerful enemies were intent on preventing his case from being placed on the court calendar for a formal trial, he decided that his only hope was for Elizabeth to go and personally plead his case before a higher authority. This she did in August 1661.

10
Chapter Ten

Elizabeth's Appeal

John Bunyan's court experiences remained clearly in his memory over the years. Some of these recollections found their way into his later writings. As a result, we know in quite some detail what occurred.

Shortly after he had been reconsigned to the Bedford Gaol, he was visited by a man named Paul Cobb. Mr. Cobb had been sent by the judges to urge Bunyan to reconsider his stance. Specifically, he demanded that Bunyan submit to the authority of the Church of England, making it clear that the judges planned to prosecute him to the full extent of the law. Mr. Cobb had no more success than the others had in getting Bunyan to change his mind, for he felt that his was the scripturally inspired position. When Cobb threatened him with being branded as a traitor, Bunyan replied that John Wycliffe had written that those who could be intimidated into not preaching God's Word would be counted as genuine traitors by Christ; and that, in any event, he was bound by his conscience to walk according to

God's laws rather than the laws of man—even those of a king.

Cobb found Bunyan to be a congenial man, but at the same time an irrational one: a true fanatic. They parted company in a friendly enough fashion, although Cobb admitted that he had succeeded only in making Bunyan's position before the law perfectly clear. As for Bunyan, he remained in prison because he had broken the law (even though it was an archaic and seldom applied law) and because he had set his heart for conscience' sake to continue to reject its authority over him.

There was clearly a cost to Bunyan because of his refusal to bend. He missed his family terribly, and felt guilty about what might befall them without his support and protection. At the beginning of his imprisonment he was tormented by the thought of death. (In Bunyan's day most of the crossroads of Europe had a gibbet upon which one could frequently see hanging the result of swift local justice. As a boy, Bunyan had seen many a body decomposing slowly on such gibbets.) The thoughts came at night to terrify him and rob him of sleep. Mr. Cobb had made it abundantly clear that such a fate most probably awaited him. He slowly overcame his concern about death but never totally overcame his fear of what his death would mean to his family, especially to his blind daughter, Mary. He wrote that such thoughts "wounded [him] to the quick" but that, in the end, he had no choice but to "venture them all with God."

Elizabeth understood well that John's only chance for liberty might rest with her. She and he worked on a petition for his freedom and she made the fifty-mile trip to London to deliver their petition to Lord Barkwood, a member of the House of Lords, who they hoped might help them. Instead of helping them, however, he referred her to the judges at Bedford.

Elizabeth returned to Bedford, resolved to present John's petitions to the judges. She received a private audience with one of the judges and gave the petition to him. Although he was somewhat sympathetic, he refused to do anything for her. She consequently approached the carriage of another judge and actually threw the petition into his carriage in order to get his attention. She did get his attention, but she also made him angry. She took another petition to the court as it sat in session, but they refused to let her speak. She tried yet one more time, appearing at a special session of the court. This time they did permit her to speak.

Finally given the opportunity to speak in behalf of her husband, she spoke with boldness and eloquence. Her position was that her husband was being illegally detained. The fact remained, however, that within the framework of the existing laws, Bunyan was being treated exactly as the regulations prescribed—indefinite imprisonment until he conformed to the state's position on church attendance and on lawful preaching.

Elizabeth's earnest presentation did not move the judges. The authorities were intent on making an example of John Bunyan. Elizabeth understood that she and her husband had no hope for help from the legal system. Their only hope was in the Lord. She sadly took the news of their petition's failure to John in the Bedford Gaol. She told him that it grieved her "to think what a sad account such poor creatures"—referring to the judiciary—"will have to give at the coming of the Lord, when they shall there answer for all things whatsoever they have done in the body." She then returned home to care for John's children and he remained imprisoned, a conscientious objector to state-controlled religion.

After Elizabeth's spirited but unsuccessful appeal in her husband's behalf, official repression did lighten a bit and Bunyan even was able to convince his jailer to permit him to make excursions outside the prison—a privilege that was not uncommon for long-standing prisoners in small, local prisons. However, when word leaked out that Bunyan was using his opportunities to preach, both he and the jailer found themselves in trouble, and Bunyan ended up being watched even more closely.

Chapter Eleven

The Prison Years

Although there is some disagreement among Bunyan's biographers, it seems likely that Bunyan spent three different terms in prison. The first was from November 1660 to the summer of 1666. The second was from the summer or autumn of 1666 to May 1672. The third was for a six-month period in 1677. The first two were served in the county prison (the Bedford Gaol), the third in the town lockup on the bridge over the river Ouse.

One thing is sure: Bunyan accepted imprisonment rather than betray his faith and his brethren. For Bunyan, however, acceptance signified neither surrender nor submission. He remained steadfastly true to his principles.

Charles II had returned from exile on May 25, 1660, landing at Dover amidst great popular acclaim and jubilation. His welcoming committee presented him with a Bible. Many people were hopeful that his return would lead to reconciliation and a lessening of religious tensions. That was not to be the case. John Bunyan was arrested on November 12, 1660.

Between 1661 and 1665 there were four separate decrees issued under the name of the Clarendon Code. This official promulgation stipulated that everyone was expected to take communion according to the rites of the Church of England; that all clergymen must be ordained by that church; and that they must agree to use the state prayer book. In addition, all religious meetings except those of the Church of England were deemed to be illegal. The final provision decreed that Nonconformist preachers could live no closer to corporate towns than a distance of five miles. If they refused to submit to the authority of the Church of England, they were in essence exiled from their places of work and worship.

The penalties for breaking any of these laws were fines, imprisonment, or even banishment. The results were inevitable. The prisons began to fill up with men who refused to conform to the Clarendon rulings. This was the case with John Bunyan's jail. He found himself suddenly surrounded with more and more men who thought as he did. The famous English diarist Samuel Pepys recorded his impression of it all in his diary: "They go like lambs without any resistance. I would to God that they would conform or be more wise and not be catched." But conform they would not, and caught they were. This turn of events affected Bunyan's life in prison in two ways. First, he had greater opportunity of practicing and perfecting his preaching. Second, some of the sermons—many of which he wrote out—were later developed into books, and so his influence spread. And there was a third result. The men who grew so close together in prison had much time in which they could pray together, discuss doctrine, and plan for the future. Many of these who studied and prayed together later ended up establishing a series of churches around the Bedford area that maintained close relationships. As is often the case, God brought good out of what man had intended for evil.

Imprisonment in the seventeenth century was a dreadful experience. Nevertheless, Bunyan did not languish in some deep, dark, dank dungeon. Instead, he was free to receive friends and family. He drew great encouragement from the frequent visits of his family and members of the Bedford church. His church brethren brought him small gifts of food, which he could add to his meager diet. They were unable, however, to help him obtain release by any legal procedure because they too came progressively under pressure from the authorities. (The congregation eventually lost their church building and were forced to hold their meetings in secret.) Furthermore, he was free to conduct worship services and to preach within the prison, and was able to study and write. (During the first six years of his imprisonment, Bunyan wrote nine books.) The other prisoners regarded him as their chaplain.

He was even able to work to help support his family by making "long tagged laces" and was sometimes temporarily excused in order to sell them to passers-by at the prison gate.

There is an interesting story told about Bunyan (who greatly enjoyed music) that illustrates the type of man he was. He had concluded he needed a project to busy himself. He decided to do something that would have a dual purpose. First, he wanted to use some of his manual skills in a worthwhile project. Second, he wanted to make something that would aid him in his worship of God. With great ingenuity and patience, he fashioned a flute out of one of the legs of his prison stool. He very carefully hollowed out the body and then used his candle flame to burn the finger holes in the body of the flute. Late at night, after the jailer had made his rounds, Bunyan would play his flute and worship God. If the jailer returned, John simply reinserted the flute into the stool.

This flute survived both Bunyan's prison stay and the succeeding years; it remains until this day as an authentic "Bunyan relic" and a testimony to his steadfast spirit.

His main preoccupations, of course, were reading and writing. Bunyan's prison library consisted of three books: the Bible, a concordance, and John Foxe's *Book of Martyrs*. Not surprisingly, his Bible was his most powerful source of comfort and consolation, but he also spent much time reading Foxe's classic. It had a mighty impact on his spirit, supplying him with a series of heroic examples. The sufferings of those martyrs made his sufferings seem slight in comparison. Bunyan's favorite among all those stories of Christians who suffered for their faith was that of John Huss, who was burned at the stake and perished singing praises to God.

Just as had been the case for the apostle Paul, Bunyan's imprisonment gave him the time to reflect and to write. Among the nine volumes that he wrote in those six initial years was his autobiography, *Grace Abounding to the Chief of Sinners*, which was published in 1666. Vera Brittain notes that "*Grace Abounding* represents John Bunyan's final freeing of himself from spiritual torment by [the act of] writing it all down. He realized that he could now remember his former fears and doubts and sad months with comfort. He said, 'They are as the head of Goliath in my hand.' He had decanted all his misery into words. The enforced monotony of prison gave him the time to think and freedom from that sense of responsibility which would have sent him, a perpetually itinerant evangelist, traveling through the countryside in search of souls to save. An inward peace and even happiness triumphed increasingly over external hardship as he read his Bible and *Book of Martyrs*, content to find himself one of so great a cloud of witnesses."

Deprived by imprisonment of the ability to

strengthen his brethren outside through his preaching, John Bunyan decided to do it via the printed page. Biographer Gwilym O. Griffith comments that Bunyan "had a flame in his soul that made Bedford gaol a lantern whereof he was the flint, shining out significantly in flashes and signals observed of all England." Like the apostle Paul, he considered himself not a victim of the repressive government that had imprisoned him but a prisoner of the Lord.

John Bunyan was released briefly from prison after *Grace Abounding* was published. He resumed his role as an evangelist in the Bedford area until he was once again arrested. He was then guarded more closely than ever. It was during this time that his blind daughter, Mary, died—a tremendous blow to Bunyan. Frank Mott Harrison tells us that "weary of this monotonous life and saddened by the loss of his child, he was able still to say, 'I have determined, the Almighty God being my help and shield, yet to suffer, and if frail life might continue so long, even till the moss shall grow upon mine eyebrows, rather than to violate my faith and principles.' "

During this second period of his prison life, Bunyan spent most of his time reading and writing. Sometimes his friends brought him books. It is believed that, among them, Bunyan had opportunity to read John Milton's epic poem *Paradise Lost*, which had been published in 1667. What effect—if any—Milton's masterpiece had on John

Bunyan, we do not know. We do know, however, that John Milton (England's greatest Puritan writer) and John Bunyan are considered linked together in a very special way in English literature. The English historian Lord Macaulay wrote: "We are not afraid to say that, though there were many clever men in England during the latter half of the seventeenth century, there were only two great creative minds. One of those minds produced the *Paradise Lost,* the other *The Pilgrim's Progress.*" It is quite unlikely that John Milton ever heard of John Bunyan. Milton was fifty-eight and ailing when *Grace Abounding* appeared. He died in 1674, four years before the publication of *The Pilgrim's Progress.*

There is a gap in Bunyan's literary output between 1666 and 1678. This gap has caused many biographers to conclude that after he finished *Grace Abounding to the Chief of Sinners* he began work on his masterpiece, *The Pilgrim's Progress.* Vera Brittain says: "It has been said that *Pilgrim's Progress* could not have been written unless *Grace Abounding,* its 'raw material,' had preceded it; and this is true: that open confession left John free to absorb his spiritual experiences and by an inner process of transformation to recreate them, as a flower grows from the seed sown in the earth."

After 1668, Bunyan's imprisonment became much less strict. He was even set free at times to go on preaching assignments outside the prison, depending on the level of local official oppression directed against Nonconformists by the government. Bunyan was named the pastor of the Bedford Baptist church somewhere between 1668 and 1671. He was officially ordained its pastor on October 21, 1671, several months before he was once again released from prison.

12

Chapter Twelve

Bishop Bunyan

In December 1671, King Charles II signed the Declaration of Religious Indulgence. This suspended the execution of penal laws in religious matters. Bunyan was released from prison shortly afterwards. There was a lot for him to do: his Bedford congregation was larger than the other Nonconformist congregations in the area, and he was now its pastor. In addition, due to his dynamic preaching, he was in constant demand as a speaker both near and far. Consequently, he once again had little time to write.

During Bunyan's years of imprisonment, the Bedford church had lost its building. They met instead in homes or in secret outdoor meetings. During that time, they were constantly spied upon and harassed (often for reward) by those who wanted to prosecute any who refused to bow the knee to the state church. Bunyan's brave stand for the truth, however, had served to strengthen the resolve of his Bedford brethren. Even before the issuing of the Declaration of Religious Indulgence, the church had decided that it wanted him to become their pastor. "None among the brethren was so fitted for the post of pastor as John Bunyan for he had shown his fitness by his endurance of persecution, by his numerous letters to the brethren and sisters who had also suffered, by his books, and above all, by his account of his spiritual conflict in *Grace Abounding*. It could not be denied that Bunyan had been clearly called by God," declares Frank Mott Harrison.

Upon his release, in May 1672, the Bedford church appointed seven men of good reputation to work with their new pastor in the surrounding villages. Together they were able to purchase a barn for their church meetings, now that it was no longer necessary to meet in secret. Bunyan applied for a license to preach and it was granted to him in September. He also secured twenty-five licenses for other men to preach, and worked to disciple them. He began to be affectionately called "Bishop Bunyan" by those whose lives he had so deeply touched.

Monica Furlong points out that "as a pastor he had to listen to people's troubles and to counsel them—as John Gifford had once counseled him in his desperate distress. There is a tender, maternal side to Bunyan, repeatedly expressed in his writings, which suggests that this must have been particularly congenial to him. He knew from firsthand experience the torments of mind and soul, and his sermons in particular reveal a great longing to help others in similar straits—to bring, in the biblical phrase he uses for one of his sermon titles, 'light to them that sit in darkness.' He had an especial sympathy for the needy and the helpless."

Bunyan devoted himself to his pastoral duties with great zeal because he was well aware that the political climate could quickly change and the church would once again suffer religious persecution. He was accurate in his assessment. Within little over five years, King Charles annulled the Declaration of Indulgence—tearing the royal seal off the document with his own hands.

It was not long before constables arrived at the home of Pastor Bunyan with a warrant signed by thirteen judges. He was once again taken off to be locked up. Unlike the two earlier times, when he was committed to the county prison, Bunyan was this time incarcerated in the Bedford town jail, a jail built into the bridge at Bedford spanning the river Ouse. With him went a rumpled manuscript, which he had begun so long ago, during his second imprisonment. It was during this third and last incarceration that Bunyan would finally find the time to finish *The Pilgrim's Progress.*

13
Chapter Thirteen

Grace Abounding and The Pilgrim's Progress

We have seen that John Bunyan's early fame came as a preacher. His most lasting impact, however, has been through his writing. "Before Bunyan found his vocation as a writer, he won it as a preacher. Writing came secondarily and consequentially," states Christopher Hill. Bunyan wrote sixty works by the time he was sixty years old. Roger Sharrock observes that "most are moral and doctrinal treatises on the conventional Puritan pattern." That is to say, they depict the horror and hopelessness of the fallen human condition and highlight the hope that is presented to the human race through the gospel. Sharrock adds: "This alternation of terror and comfort is the systole and diastole of Bunyan's religious thought."

Bunyan's style was unique for his time. He relied more than any other writer on the common life and culture of the humble country people. This struck a chord in the hearts of his readers. Bunyan drew many of the images in his books from the sights and sounds around Bedford and from his own everyday experiences. They gave his work honesty, authenticity, and solidity. For example, the image of the wayfaring traveler plays the central role in *The Pilgrim's Progress.* Bunyan himself had traveled daily all over the Bedford area plying his trade as a tinker. The Pilgrim in his great allegory carried a great burden on his back. Bunyan understood carrying a heavy burden—both spiritually and physically. He had often carried on his travels a portable anvil weighing sixty pounds. His tools may have added another twenty pounds of weight. He carried them in a sack on his back. The relief of being able to put down such a backbreaking load no doubt had very special significance to Bunyan.

Unlike many of the unlearned Puritan "mechanick" preachers, Bunyan did not strive to make a virtue out of his lack of formal learning. Instead, he simply identified with his readers on the basis of the things he knew best. He communicated with them because he identified with them, drawing inspiration from God, from his rustic roots, and from his love for people.

John Bunyan's literary reputation is founded primarily upon four major works: *Grace Abounding to the Chief of Sinners, The Pilgrim's Progress, The Life and Death of Mister Badman,* and *The Holy War.* Many count the latter two as works of genius and the former two as works of surpassing genius. We shall in passing only briefly consider *Grace Abounding* and *The Pilgrim's Progress,* his best known works. Neither work would likely ever have been written except for Bunyan's imprisonments between 1660 and 1672, so busy was he with his evangelistic duties. At the time of his final arrest and imprisonment, his reputation as a preacher had already spread far and wide. He was constantly being invited to places to preach.

Bunyan kept working at his craft in prison. It is believed that *Grace Abounding* originally came out of his testifying to groups of people in and around Bedford about his inner spiritual journey. This was accepted Puritan practice: to share with others in public meetings an account of the trials and victories involved with coming to a position of rest (assurance) in the Lord. The enforced idleness and solitude of his prison years had forced him to reevaluate his life and ministry. He wrote out his spiritual autobiography primarily to encourage, guide, and comfort his brethren outside prison. The dramatic impact of this work came from his evangelistic bent and his desire to touch hearts with the story of God's saving grace. Biographical details are scant simply because Bunyan did not regard the details of his life as important; he believed that his story was important only as a spiritual encouragement to others. Biographer Frank Mott Harrison concludes that Bunyan "possessed God-given creative genius which enabled him to paint in words the picture of his own life—nay, of any life."

Bunyan worked diligently to find a way to picture in words the intense inner dealings of God so that others might profit thereby. Roger Sharrock explains: "When Bunyan came to write *The Pilgrim's Progress,* he had only to translate his own spiritual odyssey into an allegory." Biographer Lynn Veach Sadler agrees that "the genesis of Bunyan's literary works is to be found in his Puritan religious experience." John Bunyan's Puritan experience was one of both head and heart. It was primarily through his writings (especially through *The Pilgrim's Progress*) that the Puritan spirit entered the mainstream of English thought.

The form and subject matter of *Grace Abounding* were not unique. They belong rather to a large class of Puritan autobiographies written in the seventeenth century. The Puritans were an introspective lot and tended to keep in their personal diaries voluminous and minute observations of the spiritual state of their souls. They emphasized God's grace: how He brought them to understand that their attempts to establish a righteousness of their own was futile; that such self-made righteousness was seen by the Lord as "filthy rags." They followed the leadings and callings of the Lord into an assurance of election, based upon their understanding of a righteousness imputed to them by God on the basis of faith in the completed work of Jesus Christ. It was not usually a quick process. Samuel Willard describes it this way: "God's decree of election may run underground a great while before it rises and breaks out in an effectual calling." This is the stuff of which *Grace Abounding* was made.

Christopher Hill writes that Bunyan "was a representative Puritan artisan who happened to be a writer of genius, a creative artist of dissent. He was also passionately, fiercely, and theologically on the side of the poor." Bunyan's preaching and then his writing did tend to cause insecurity among those who clung so stubbornly to the status quo. In this, Bunyan drew inspiration from those who had risked much to preach the gospel during England's turbulent history: from the Lollards, from Bilney, Ridley, Hooper and Cranmer. A clear current of nostalgia exists in Bunyan's writings. He was a voice for the poor and for the spiritually hungry. It is not accidental that the evil characters in *The Pilgrim's Progress* are all carefully described as lords and gentlemen. Bunyan's Christianity had both an eternal perspective and a social conscience. Puritans always made a clear distinction between "talkers" and "doers."

Bunyan, of course, had no idea that he was writing a masterpiece of literature as he penned *The Pilgrim's Progress*. He was simply following the leading of the Lord as he understood it. He knew very little about literature apart from the Bible, but he certainly did know his Bible. Bunyan, in fact, wrote, "My Bible and concordance are my only library in my writings. I depend on the sayings of no man. I found my doctrine in the Scriptures of Truth, among the true sayings of God." The highly poetic King James version of the Bible had appeared only seventeen years before his birth. It was in this Bible (itself a masterpiece of English prose) that Bunyan lived until its words became his own.

Bunyan thus vividly coupled his own spiritual experiences (becoming a sort of Everyman) with inspired, biblical prose. Bunyan's dramatic style and dramatic success helped pave the way for a new kind of literature: the novel. Some critics consider him the father of the English novel. As for Bunyan, Vera Brittain notes, "he neither knew nor cared that at a single step he had created the English novel, with its long history and infinite variety. Still less did it matter to him that, in time to come, he would be an honored member of those 'English Men of Letters' whose contemporary representatives were either to remain genuinely unaware of him or to display ostentatious indifference. His sole purpose was to bring sinners to repentance; to 'conduct the weak and tempted people of God,' for whose benefit he had already published *Grace Abounding*, on a pilgrimage through the wilderness of this world to the glory of that which is to come.

"The popularity of *The Pilgrim's Progress* with the unpretentious is easily understood. Religious books were then almost the only serious reading among the poor, and this one represented their struggles, ideals, and emotions in the form of a story vivid in color and enthralling in action. The widely held conception of life as a pilgrimage derived its images from the Bible rather than from other sources."

Bunyan would have been quite unimpressed with being considered by some to have been the father of the English novel because Bunyan had a heavenly, not an earthly vision. He wrote primarily not to entertain but to instruct, to comfort, and to edify. Dr. Martyn Lloyd-Jones has written that Bunyan was "a preacher, a pastor, a man who, because of terrible experiences through which he passed, had a profound concern of soul for the ordinary man and woman, and Christian people in particular. If Bunyan and his writings were God's gift to the world of men and of literature, it is even more true that they were a special gift to the church. Bunyan could truly say (as the apostle Paul had said before him) that he was not disobedient to the heavenly vision."

14
Chapter Fourteen

The Jail on the River

The third time he was arrested, Bunyan was not taken as before to the county jail. This time he was placed in the Bedford town jail, a jail which was built into the bridge which spanned the river Ouse. It was a dreadful place, dark and dank. Disappointment weighed heavily upon him. He was once again deprived of his freedom, his family, and of the joy his pastoral duties brought him. He was not, however, deprived of the comforting fellowship of his God nor of His call upon his life. Bunyan determined that he would write in order to edify those he had left behind and to fruitfully pass the time. He had written much during his first incarceration and had studied much during his second term in prison. He was about to put the efforts of both time periods in his life to good and fruitful use. Bunyan was about to complete his masterpiece, *The Pilgrim's Progress.*

There is some difference of opinion among Bunyan biographers concerning both the exact time when *The Pilgrim's Progress* was written and where it was written. Some feel it was begun during his second imprisonment (the Bedford Gaol) and completed during his third imprisonment in the little jail on the bridge. Others feel it was begun as well as completed during his final imprisonment. We *do* know for certain that it was finished by early in 1678.

The story of its genesis is by now quite famous. Bunyan explains that one night he fell into a fitful sleep and had an extraordinary dream. The dream was so vivid that its details were impressed firmly on his mind and heart. Even when he was fully awake, the dream remained more real in a way than his prison surroundings. It so seized upon his imagination that he felt constrained to write it all down. Whenever he tried to take up his pen to work on something else, the dream again overwhelmed him, and he set to work once more recording what he had so clearly seen. The days melded together. Bunyan himself was often taken aback by the strength and clarity of his vision. He nevertheless struggled with this strange project—a project that he for a while considered frivolous. He tried to force himself to concentrate upon more serious and scholarly works. He set himself, for example, to writing a treatise that would explain and clarify his biblical principles, hoping that this work might convince his captors and opponents that he was no danger to the state. Even so, he kept returning to his allegory.

By the end of 1671, we know, he had completed his theological work, titled *A Confession of My Faith: And a Reason for My Practice*, and a large stack of manuscript pages in which he had related his dream. It appears that once he was set free from prison in 1672, he worked only sporadically on what was to become *The Pilgrim's Progress* until he was once again imprisoned. When he started to work on it again in his small cell on the River Ouse, he began to hope that it might indeed be more than just a fairy tale. He began to believe, in fact, that his stirring allegory might minister the truths of salvation in a different way and to a different group than his more serious books could do.

Once on paper, this book became one of the most-read books in world history. Frank Mott Harrison states that "*The Pilgrim's Progress* is a whole-length portrait of Bunyan himself. His dream-story has been translated into a hundred and twenty or more languages and dialects (more than any other book, save the Bible)." He adds that "an old divine with truth has said: 'God gave a great gift to the Church of Christ throughout the world, and to the English-speaking people in particular, when He created and converted John Bunyan to compose *The Pilgrim's Progress*.'"

Despite the King's disposition regarding Dissenters, the religious and political climate in England was continuing to change. His repressive policies eventually became untenable. And so, after about six months, Bunyan was again released from prison—this time permanently. He had become the anvil upon which many hammers were ultimately worn out. His reputation as a righteous man had continued to grow—spread throughout England by his writings. He had outlasted his captors.

These months in jail had not been wasted. Bunyan had set aside other writing projects in order to finish recording his dramatic dream. When he completed the work, he consulted with visiting friends about its publication. They were divided in their opinion. Some were for doing so, some against it. Bunyan decided that, lacking clear direction, he would follow what he believed the leading of the Lord to be. He therefore submitted it to his friend at Cambridge, the great Puritan preacher John Owen. Owen encouraged him to publish it, which he did. *The Pilgrim's Progress* became an instant success, going through more than a dozen printings in ten years, selling more than one hundred thousand copies in Great Britain alone.

Having now been released from jail, Bunyan put aside all writing for the next three or four years, concentrating on his flock, preaching and carrying out other church duties. The power of his preaching continued to flourish as he studied and perfected it. Eventually he went back to his writing, producing *The Holy War* and, in 1684, the second part of *The Pilgrim's Progress* (the journey of Christiana and her children) as well as other lesser-known works.

Monica Furlong is of the opinion that "the tone of *Pilgrim's Progress* (especially the second part) is more cheerful, humorous, and hopeful than *Grace Abounding*." She believes that Bunyan had come to a place of balance in his theology and in his life, a place of confidence and joy.

When Bunyan was released from the Bedford jail, he had less than eleven more years to live. He would remain free for the rest of his life and busy in the service of the Lord. He continued to preach, to pastor, and to write. He was also often called upon by brethren in nearby congregations to arbitrate in a variety of difficult issues of church life. His talents in dealing with people cost him many a long, hard journey. Ola Elizabeth Winslow has written that "in the end, it would cost him his life, but even had he known, he would have still gone willingly and with a sense of duty laid on him by God Himself."

15

Chapter Fifteen

The Years of Triumph

Biographer Vera Brittain writes that "the mature prisoner who came out of the Bedford Gaol in May 1672 did not even physically resemble the young man who had entered the prison in November 1660. His face, framed in long auburn hair, had then been ruddy in tone, and healthily bronzed from perpetual riding and tramping in the open air. His eyes, lively as a blue candle-flame, held a latent hint of gaiety even when he was praying or preaching. Twelve years afterwards, though he was still no more than forty-three, gray threads appeared in the bronze hair, cut short like that of his fellow prisoners. The puffiness of his flesh reflected the interminable hours spent in darkness; the deep lines beneath his eyes emphasized their grave reflectiveness, half visionary and half reminiscent. He had that air of authority which men and women acquire who have been through deep waters of experience and come out victorious. Yet, if he lived for another thirty years, he would never forget the fetid stench of the rat-infested dungeon beneath the gaol; the raucous quarrels of detained felons; the vicious practices of long-term prisoners cut off from normal living; the dirt and the lice; the cruelty and corruption of some of his jailers."

Monica Furlong believes that in 1677 Bunyan came out of prison as a hero. She writes: "Mankind loves a man who has suffered for a cause and survived, even if they do not care for the cause and would not dream of suffering for it themselves. They were glad to identify with those who had behaved as well as they would have liked to have done themselves. Bunyan was a ready-made hero, not only because he had bravely endured a harsh term of imprisonment or because his cheerful, sturdy character was much to the English taste, but also because he had made himself known to a huge public by writing the first part of *The Pilgrim's Progress.*"

John Bunyan had another decade to live. Ironically, it would be a stormy time for England and a time of relative tranquillity for him. His reputation had grown during his years in prison. People respected him for his willingness to suffer for what he believed. The success of *The Pilgrim's Progress* created a great demand for his other works. His fame had spread far beyond Bedford. He was now a preacher much in demand, making trips on horseback to London and beyond. He rode forth from Bedford to minister to others, clearly unconcerned about either fame or fortune. One of Bunyan's contemporaries wrote of him that "he was not a man who preached by way of bargain for money, for he hath refused a more plentiful income to keep his station." These were years, then, of preaching, teaching, traveling, counseling, visiting and writing. In the last decade of his life he wrote thirty-six pieces of publishable writing—thirty-four of which found their way into print. The most notable of these was the second part of *The Pilgrim's Progress.* Vera Brittain concludes that this great work and the others of lesser magnitude that he wrote "made their contribution to that task of soul-salvation which in John's eyes was so much more important than literary achievement."

Although England was beset by all manner of political considerations and struggles, Bunyan kept his hand to the plow, remaining faithful—as the apostle Paul said—"to the heavenly vision." With each passing year he drew closer to the end of his commission. He had "endured hardship, done the work of an evangelist, and fulfilled his ministry." He was already being "poured out as a drink offering. The time of his departure had come. He had fought the good fight and finished the course. He had kept the faith, knowing that there was laid up for him a crown of righteousness, which the Lord, the righteous Judge, would award to him on that day" (2 Timothy 4:5–8).

In the second half of *The Pilgrim's Progress,* Bunyan wrote some words about the end of

Christiana's journey—words that could well have described the end of his own journey: "The Waters are to the Palate bitter, and to the Stomack cold; yet the thoughts of what I am going to, and the Conduct that waits for me on the other side doth lie as a glowing Coal at my heart." Monica Furlong describes Bunyan's last years this way: "Within four years of writing these lines Bunyan himself was dead, and they are the best of epitaphs for him, as the whole book is the best portrait of Bunyan's character, and in particular of the contentment of the last ten years of his life. It is the contentment of a man who has found liberation, particularly from fear and depression, and who has made peace with his own conscience. It is a contentment too which owes much to happy human relationship, not only, as we may guess, to the pleasure of children and grandchildren, but also the pleasure of a warm and loving Christian community in which he has a secure and respected identity. He seems untouched by disillusion, although he has a realistic sense of what the problems of belief are; it is as if, having been delivered from the shattering conflicts that beset his youth, he can never again lose hope."

Chapter Sixteen

16

Death

The death of John Bunyan came suddenly, unexpectedly, and—in the world's eyes—prematurely. It all began when he went out in a pelting rain to preach as usual to his congregation and to minister communion. He returned home after the church service to work on a manuscript that he was preparing for publication. His studies were interrupted by a visitor who urgently wanted to speak with him. The young man, a type of prodigal son, was one whose behavior had estranged him from his father. Bunyan opened his heart and the Scriptures to him, bringing comfort by pointing him to the love of God and leading him to scriptural repentance. The young man then asked Bunyan to visit his father who had closed his door and his heart to him. He agreed to visit the father before pushing on to London to preach and to deliver his new manuscript.

Bunyan went by horseback to Reading where he accomplished two tasks in the name of the Lord. He knocked on the door of the father of the young prodigal son in an effort to bring reconciliation between them. Jesus Christ knocked on the door of the man's heart—and in a flood of tears the old man was reconciled with God and with his son. John Bunyan then preached a stirring message to the church at Reading. He stayed up late talking with the pastor of the church. The next morning was gray and there was a threat of rain. His friends from Reading tried to prevail upon him to postpone his departure, but he was eager to push on to London, a trip of more than forty miles.

Bunyan arrived in London fatigued and soaked to the skin. He went to bed and slept a feverish sleep. He should have remained in bed to rest, but insisted instead on preaching as he had come to do. The text for his final sermon was 1 John 1:13. History records that it was a sermon "gentle in admonition, positive in tone, and with an intimacy in address." He returned home from church even more ill. He went to bed but grew steadily worse. Neither Bunyan nor his friends realized at first how seriously ill he really was, otherwise he would have sent for his devoted Elizabeth to be with him. The infection worsened quickly due to his weakened physical condition and because he had for so long persistently overworked himself. Toward the end, his friends gathered at his bedside. When they asked him how they could comfort him, Bunyan responded, "I desire nothing more than to be with Christ, which is far better." He soon grew delirious. His thoughts traveled far from the London bedroom in which he was dying. He thought constantly of Elizabeth, and of his blind daughter, Mary, that beloved eldest child whose death during his prison years had deepened the shadows of his night. He also remembered his sister Margaret, the playmate of his youth, with whom he had sat fishing on the banks of the Ouse and had explored the fields around Elstow. Vera Brittain writes that as he finally lapsed into unconsciousness "his dreams took flight to the place that throughout his life as a preacher and pastor had been identified with the liberation from the burden of sin." The Pilgrim was finally ready to enter the Celestial City. Bunyan died twelve days later, on August 31, 1688, three months short of his sixtieth birthday.

Elizabeth Bunyan had felt strangely unsettled about her dear husband's trip. When the letter from London arrived, Elizabeth's worst fears were confirmed. She had stood beside her husband in good times and bad. Their steadfast devotion to each other had always made even the worst times more bearable. Vera Brittain says that "she had lived for him and his children, and the news dealt her a blow as mortal as the rainstorm had inflicted on John. Though she was still under fifty, she survived him only long enough to see his affairs left in order, and made arrangements for the publication of his remaining manuscripts."

The news of Bunyan's passing dealt a tremendous blow to the Bedford church; a blow compounded somehow in that he had breathed his last breath so far from home and those who loved him. The church set aside a day for prayer and fasting. It would be three full years before they appointed another pastor.

Bunyan left no worldly wealth behind him. His wife lived—until she went to join her husband in the presence of the Lord—on the sale of their modest goods and the small profit then available to authors for their works.

He was laid to rest in a field which eventually became known as Bunhill Fields. This verse was inscribed on his original gravestone:

"The Pilgrim's Progress now is finished,
And death has laid him in his earthly bed."

17
Chapter Seventeen

Conclusion

John Bunyan's life spanned one of the most tumultuous periods in English history. It was a time of political and religious upheaval. It was a time during which the Puritans rose to power in England, toppling a King from his throne and replacing him with a Protector (Oliver Cromwell) after a bloody civil war. It was a time when religious oppression turned to religious freedom and then back again, several times. It was also a time of religious fervor. Many people—including both Oliver Cromwell and John Bunyan—expected the soon return of the Lord. Christopher Hill has perceptively declared: "Cromwell aimed to bring about the Kingdom of God on Earth and instead founded the British Empire. Bunyan wanted the Millennium and got the novel instead."

It was also a time when English religious history was changed forever: a time that reaped the harvest of all those who had been willing to suffer persecution for righteousness' sake for so many years. Among these men was John Bunyan. He stood his ground for religious freedom amidst state persecution and threats of death, helping to guarantee the right of freedom of conscience for all Englishmen. He bravely and fruitfully faced more than twelve difficult years of imprisonment so that others might worship as they chose.

In a sense, Bunyan represented and symbolized all the faithful Dissenters who took the same stand that he did. He stood his ground until the climate of thought in England changed. And Bunyan changed too. Vera Brittain observes that during his lifetime "he passed through the whole gamut of opinion from Calvinistic intolerance to the larger charity which carried England into an era of religious toleration." In a sense, he outlasted his tormentors, for in the end Charles II recognized that all the government efforts during the years Bunyan spent imprisoned were of no avail. Bunyan was thus an unusual man who lived in an unusual time. Although his life and work clearly had political impact, he was not a political man. He saw his mission to be a spiritual one. His focus was not on earthly things but on heavenly things. "His compass was set to no goal possible to human achievement and to no rewards of man's bestowal," declared Ola Elizabeth Winslow.

Unaffected in his heart by all that the world so highly esteems, Bunyan was nevertheless used by God to make a mark on history. Seeking to remain unshaped by the philosophies of man, he rather became a shaper of English thought. Ms. Winslow writes that "by the singleness of his own individual conviction . . . he made articulate what thousands of ordinary men and women of his day believed, dreamed, hoped for, responded to, in things religious. He forged out a path of a religious quest which became a main track for the following century. He helped to shape the cultural pattern of his own day and the day immediately after. The story of English Puritanism can hardly be understood without his contribution to the record. It is the common man's contribution."

The mystery of John Bunyan can best be understood by considering two things: his God-given genius and his godly calling. Bunyan's genius rests perhaps on his universality. R. Ellis Roberts stated that "we value him first not for what he tells us of his own day, his own religion or his own society, but for what he tells us of ours." As a man, Bunyan's experiences as a Puritan dissenter were more typical than unique. What *was* unique about Bunyan was how God chose to use him. Bunyan is a "mystery" in the biblical meaning of the word. In the New Testament, a mystery is something that remains hidden until God chooses to reveal it. It was God's working in Bunyan's life, His inspiration and energizing power, that made Bunyan and his work a revelation and an inspiration to men. God's favorite method, after all, for touching the lives of people is . . . other people. Bunyan's life and message were so powerful exactly because God used him as a representative of mankind. He was himself the man he described in *The Pilgrim's Progress*—"the man clothed with rags, standing in a certain place, a book in his hand and a great burden on his back." Ola E. Winslow further adds that "his own life story is disarmingly simple, but for all that (and perhaps because of it) there is a strong human pull to it. Bunyan contributed no new theological ideas; he led no movement; he fired men as individuals, not as followers. He was original in that he translated a complex system of theology into a way of life simple enough to be understood by the least taught of those who listened. He was original in that a fire burned in him that kindled a fire in other men."

Although Bunyan was a powerful and popular preacher during his time, his true legacy to England and to the world was his writing. The famous English romantic poet Samuel Coleridge wrote this about Bunyan and *The Pilgrim's Progress*: "I know of no book, the Bible excepted, as above all comparison, which I, according to my judgment and experience, could so safely recommend as teaching and enforcing the whole saving truth according to the mind that was in Christ Jesus, as *The Pilgrim's Progress*." That was Bunyan's goal, his mission: to point out the way of salvation to people so that they might understand it clearly and embrace it eagerly.

Bunyan, the man on a mission, completed his mission in Christ. Like the apostle Paul, he could write, "I have fought the good fight, I have finished the course, I have kept the faith." We can be sure that—as is true for Paul—there was laid up for him the crown of righteousness, which the Lord, the righteous Judge, will award to him on that day; and not only to him, but also to all who have loved His appearing.

18

Chapter Eighteen

An Allegory of My Own

"To bring out prisoners from the dungeon,
And those who dwell in darkness from the prison.
I am the LORD, that is My name." (Isa. 42:7–8)

"To hear the groaning of the prisoner;
to set free those who were doomed to death." (Ps. 102:20)

"The LORD sets the prisoners free." (Ps. 146:7)

Frederick Langbridge penned this following perceptive couplet:

"Two men look out through the same bars:
One sees the mud, and one the stars."

Alister McGrath offered the following explanation of Langbridge's observation: "It is quite possible for two people to be in exactly the same situation and yet see it in quite different ways. Two men, looking out through the same prison bars, may see very different things. One looks down and sees the mud; the other lifts his eyes to heaven, and sees the stars. The point that

Langbridge is trying to make is that some people see nothing but the rut of everyday life, ending in death, while others raise their eyes to heaven, knowing that their ultimate destiny lies with God." The latter was the case with John Bunyan.

Bunyan's prison years did not break him. Instead, they served to mold and refine him. His focus during those years was not on his own suffering and misery but on the principles of sacrifice, fellowship with God, spiritual growth, and service. Bunyan believed that although his body was imprisoned, the Word of God was not. More than by any other thing, his prison years were defined by his Bible study—and by the books that were inspired by that study. In the following little allegory, three types of men endure exactly the same prison experience. But their response to their imprisonment is based on their response to God's Word.

• • •

Once upon a time there were three prisoners. Imprisoned were they in the deepest and darkest part of the most terrible dungeon that has ever existed. Their captor was the most cruel and most powerful of jailers who has ever lived. No escape was possible. Consequently, they had no hope. All that existed for the three wretched prisoners in this harsh house of bondage was misery, pain, and groaning—and loneliness, even in their shared cell.

The prisoners sat dejected and silent in their

cold, dark cell, day after lonely day. They exchanged neither words nor smiles, isolated in their individual suffering. They had lived this way for—it seemed—countless days and nights.

Suddenly, one momentous day, things changed! The oppressive silence in their cell was shattered by a mighty shout and the tremendous, majestic sounding of a trumpet. The trumpet's blaring seemed to sound and resound again and again off the walls of the cell. Then the rusty locks on the massive cell door began to give way. The hinges cried shrilly as the door swung slowly open. The prisoners buried their faces in their hands as a sudden and powerful light pierced the darkness, striking eyes unaccustomed to such brilliance.

Peering between their fingers, they could discern the form of a man standing before them. They had no idea who this one might be, for they had never seen him before—but he was most assuredly a man of great power and authority, a person of might, valor, and royal demeanor. He produced a golden key and unlocked the chains that shackled them to the cold wall. With a voice of authority and compassion he declared: "The dark lord who has held you captive for so long has been overthrown. You are now free to depart if you will recognize the lordship of the One who has overcome your jailer, for it is His loving desire that you choose to serve Him alone. If you are indeed willing to trust and serve Him, you may proceed to His palace and meet this Great King. You may even dwell with Him there if you elect to do so, and be treated as a prince—with all the rank, privileges, power, and authority of royalty. All you need do is to respond in obedience to the truth that you have now heard."

Suddenly, he was gone as quickly as he had come. The door to the cell, however, remained open. The three men were at first too stunned to react. Slowly and timidly, they began to discuss what they had seen and heard. The oldest prisoner, he who had been there the longest, was the first to speak. He moaned, "I cannot go. I have grown used to my chains. Change frightens me more than chains. This is the only life I have ever known. To believe that what this man tells us is true is impossible! It is all too easy. Life is hard. Things like this just don't happen, especially to me. It must be a trick! I cannot go. I *will* not go. Perhaps, some day, I may manage to find a way of escape on my own." And he did not go. No amount of discussion, persuasion, reasoning, or pleading could change his mind. As far as we know, he remains in that prison to this very day. Perhaps he died there.

The second prisoner declared, "I believe it *is* true! I am leaving this vile place!" With that, he jumped up, shook off his chains, and hurried through the open door. He ran into the nearby village—a pleasant place. He lived out the rest of his life there in relative comfort. He did not venture on to the King's palace because he did not know what might be expected of him there. The story about living there as a prince seemed far too good to be true. He knew he did not deserve that—and never could—and did not wish to risk losing what he had already gained. He decided to accept what seemed refreshing and good to him. But in so doing, he lost out on the best. He lived out his life with little impact on people around him. Rarely did he speak to anyone about how he had been liberated from prison. He almost never shared with the villagers what he had heard about the Great King.

The third prisoner walked deliberately through the open cell door and journeyed on to the nearby village. But he kept going; he walked resolutely on to the palace of the Great King, the King of kings. He presented himself at the gate on the basis of the truth he had heard in prison—and which he believed to be true. His was a royal welcome! He was given a new, shining robe to wear, and a signet ring of authority was placed on his finger. Then he was warmly received into the household of the King. He lived for the rest of his days in loving fellowship with the King himself and with others of His royal family. He loved them all more each day, and he served the King well—loyally, fruitfully, and faithfully. It was, in fact, his greatest joy to serve his King and to have continuous fellowship with Him. He was given royal authority to go forth in the name of his King to visit terrible prisons—dungeons like the one where he had languished for so long and in which he had first heard the Good News. He proclaimed to others the same message of freedom that he himself had heard and believed. He, too, blew great and majestic blasts on his golden trumpet, announcing the freedom truth brings. And the many who believed the truth were indeed set free.

• • •

Truth applied brings freedom! This is the glorious message of the Church. He whom the Son sets free is free indeed (John 8:31–36)! This is the message that dominated the life and work of John Bunyan.

I shall end this look at the life of John Bunyan with two more illuminating and defining quotes from Monica Furlong: "Bunyan was like a prisoner who is saved at the last moment when he has given up all hope of his life, and he can never get over the sense of gratitude and joy in living with which this unexpected liberation has filled him." In short, John Bunyan wrote what he lived. She concludes: "The experiential level is what gives so much of Bunyan's work a warmth and vitality that makes it readable today. He describes in *Grace Abounding* going to church in a state of despair at his own sinfulness, convinced he is bound for hell. The preacher speaks of the love of Christ for man, and moved by his words Bunyan hears a voice within him say, 'Thou art my

Love, thou art my Love; and nothing shall separate thee from my love.' Throughout his life he never 'got over' the sense of wonder at the forgiveness and healing he had received."

That was—and is—the heart of Bunyan's message.

Bibliography

Brittain, Vera. *Valiant Pilgrim*. New York: The Macmillan Company, 1950.

Firth, Charles. *Cromwell's Army: A History of the English Soldiers During the Civil Wars*. London: Greenhill Books, Ltd., 1992.

Furlong, Monica. *Puritan's Progress*. New York: Coward, McCann, and Geoghegan, Inc., 1975.

Griffith, Gwilym O. *John Bunyan*. London: Hodder and Stoughton, 1977.

Harrison, Frank Mott. *John Bunyan*. Carlisle, Pennsylvania: The Banner of Truth Trust, 1964.

Hill, Christopher. *A Tinker and a Poor Man: John Bunyan and His Church, 1628–1688*. New York: Alfred A. Knopf, 1989.

Sadler, Lynn Veach. *John Bunyan*. Boston: Twayne Publishers, 1979.

Sharrock, Roger. *John Bunyan*. New York: St. Martin's Press, 1968.

Talon, Henri A. *John Bunyan: The Man and His Works*. London: Longmans, Green and Company, 1956.

Winslow, Ola Elizabeth. *John Bunyan*. New York: The Macmillan Company, 1961.

This book was produced by the Christian Literature Crusade. We hope it has been helpful to you in living the Christian life. CLC is a literature mission with ministry in over 50 countries worldwide. If you would like to know more about us, or are interested in opportunities to serve with a faith mission, we invite you to write to:

Christian Literature Crusade
P.O. Box 1449
Fort Washington, PA 19034
U.S.A.